The Ultimate Guide to
Mad Men

About the author

Will Dean is staff writer on the Guardian Guide.

He was sold on Mad Men as soon as Don Draper
opened his desk drawer to reveal a collection
of immaculately dry-cleaned shirts.

His favourite book is Billy Liar
by Keith Waterhouse.

Originally from Oldham, he now lives in
north London with his girlfriend and a badly
maintained bicycle. This is his first book.

MAY   2011

The Ultimate Guide to

Mad Men

Will Dean

guardianbooks

Published by Guardian Books 2010

4 6 8 10 9 7 5 3

Copyright © Guardian News and Media Ltd 2010

First published in Great Britain in 2010 by
Guardian Books
Kings Place, 90 York Way
London N1 9GU

www.guardianbooks.co.uk

A CIP catalogue record for this book
is available from the British Library

ISBN 978-0-85265-233-6

Typeset by seagulls.net
Printed and bound in Great Britain by CPI Bookmarque

Contents

Foreword

Mad Men is a show about advertising in the same way that the Sopranos is a show about the mafia. Or that The Wire is a show about drug dealing. At its root, yes, this is a drama centred around a smokey, cynical advertising agency beginning. But advertising is used solely as a prism through which we can look at the world, in this case the axis-shifting period of the early 1960s.

From the politics of the Nixon/Kennedy race in 1960 to the health effects of smoking; from the still simmering battle against communism to the burgeoning Civil Rights movement, Mad Men's genius isn't to tell us what we already know about these things, it's to show us how people might have reacted to them. Especially people in high-powered Madison Avenue jobs who assumed a degree of omnipotence. In most instances, it's to hardly notice and to idly watch as a new world wraps itself around the drama of their lives.

In fact, one of the real pleasures of the show is watching the slow unravelling of the main players at Sterling Cooper. We meet them when they are – to borrow Tom Wolfe's phrase – early Masters Of The Universe. They move from ten martini lunches to dinners at New York's most exclusive restaurants, absolutely assured that the status quo – their status quo – will perpetuate. Meanwhile, the viewer is gifted the benefit of watching with the 20/20 hindsight of 50 years of political, sexual, medical and cultural progress. But the real genius of the writing is that we can understand the characters' prejudices and their ignorance. Yet we also recognise those, like Peggy Olson, who are willing to challenge the world that has been spun out before them.

Mad Men begins on a cultural precipice. In its fashions, customs and even styles, it's the world of the late 1950s that we're looking at. The world outside has already started to change, but for the Roger Sterlings of that world – they've barely even noticed. Watching things slowly catch up with them is a tremendously satisfying ride.

My own personal satisfaction while watching the show was helped enormously by being asked to write a series of episode by episode blogs for guardian.co.uk in which I would share a brief recap and a few talking points with readers. It quickly became a part of the routine of watching the series for many viewers eager to share their thoughts.

In his book about advertising, From Those Wonderful Folks Who Gave You Pearl Harbour, legendary creative Jerry Della Femina (See page 76) talks about going to London with an idea to perhaps try and take over Saatchi & Saatchi. Having made his way into the Saatchi offices, he quickly realises that the men and women there know so much more than him and that he has to make a dash for it before they buy his firm.

So, when I idly started writing a thousand words' worth of reflections and minor points on Mad Men at the beginning of the show's second series in the UK, I had no idea of the level of fervour and enthusiasm with which commenters would dissect the show. The people watching it saw more and absorbed more than any other TV show I've ever watched. It was fantastic, a stroll through the Saatchi offices wouldn't do.

And so began a crowdsourced analysis of the show, which grew each and every week – meaning every minor detail embedded by the writers was picked up on by hundreds of pairs of eyes. Mad Men is by far the most wonderfully multi-layered show on television – watching it with a group so clever, cutting and analytical as the Notes From The Break Room blog contributors made it even better and made this book possible. So thank-you to everyone who commented over the course of the first three seasons – if all of your great words and observations had been used this book would be longer than Bert Cooper's favourite, Atlas Shrugged. I'm sorry it can't be.

Thank-you in particular to the most regular commenters and all those included here: JoeDoone, DellaMirandola, Nevada, Bella79, Oldmuskrat, ArundelXVI, Zanina, Superspartan, Berkowit28, BlueWillow, Discussant, Waifandstray, BashaL, Tess61, Dominia, KeithyD, RiverAngel, PaulJamesG, TheKevster, RockNRollMassacre, DogManStar, Tess61, Insomniac506, PureImagination, CareFree, Mike65ie, IceniQueen, MacEasy, Sansucre, NoseyRosie, JReid, UninspiredName, ElectricDragon, Promethea, SexedUp, Avian, Horatio93, AlexJones, RoyHudd, LEA3012, PhelimONeill, UncleSchnorbitz, MissBean, AQuietMAn, SaintSnowy, DoraVale, LucyT, DrQuinzel, HerrDobler, CrashBoomBang, Smee, Kinetic, Shov, GoddessInTheBlueSari and JJ139. Apologies to anyone I've missed out.

Some personal thanks: First, to all the writers from the Guardian and Observer for allowing us to reproduce their fine work here; to Alex Needham for asking me to start the blog; all the people who've helped edit it including Paul MacInnes, Oginia O'Dell, James Anthony, Dugald Baird and Peter Robins; to Lisa Darnell for suggesting the book; to Malik Meer and Richard Vine for proof-reading and guidance; a huge thanks to Vicky Frost and Tim Lusher for supervising the blogs and taking on the extra work to put up series one; to my mum for getting into the spirit of things by buying the Mad Men DVDs and ringing up with suggestions; to Gemma for putting up with me being glued to the laptop rather than leaving the flat and most importantly to Matthew Weiner and the entire cast and crew of Mad Men for making a show so brilliant that five books like this wouldn't do it justice.

Will Dean, London, July 2010

The unedited Notes From The Break Room is online at:
guardian.co.uk/culture/series/notes-from-the-break-room

Editor's note

The episode-by-episode blogs for seasons two and three were published "live", ie they went online just after the episodes had broadcast on BBC4 in the United Kingdom*. As such, both the main posts and the discussions following them are unaware as to what is coming later in the series and spoiler free, so can be read along with the series if you are watching it for the first time.

The blogs themselves were/are intended to be general recaps with setting off points for discussion below the line. Highlights of those discussions are included here with each episode.

*Series one was blogged retrospectively in spring 2010.

A show so good you'd be willing to trade body parts for a sneak preview

CHARLIE BROOKER SALUTES MAD MEN

Mad Men is one of those rare shows you just don't want to end. Thankfully its pace is so languid, it almost doesn't start, let alone finish. 85% of each episode consists of Don Draper staring into the middle distance through a veil of cigarette smoke. Sometimes so little appears to be happening, you have to fight the urge to get up and slap your TV to make the characters start moving again. Hypnotic visuals, lingering pace: Mad Men is television's very own lava lamp. I'm exaggerating, of course, as anyone who's been absorbing the show on a season-by-season basis will attest. And I use the word "absorb" deliberately: you don't really "watch" Mad Men: you lie back and let it seep into you. It works by osmosis.

David Simon once explained The Wire's deliberate refusal to decode cop jargon and street lingo was a conscious ploy to force the viewer to "lean in"; to make an effort, to engage, to pay close attention to the dialogue. Mad Men plays things differently. It makes the viewer lean back. The programme's glacial tempo is startlingly alien to the average modern viewer, accustomed to meaningless televisual lightshows such as CSI

Miami – all winking lights and trick shots and musical montages telling you what to think with such detached efficiency they might as well issue a bullet-pointed list of plot points and moods and have done with it. Shows in which the story is secondary to the edit, edit, edit: where any sense of meaning or even authentic emotion is doomed to death by a million tiny cuts. Mad Men's tranquility and poise makes it resemble a still photograph by comparison. The viewer has to calm the fuck down to even start appreciating it.

But the notion that nothing happens in Mad Men is bullshit. Every scene has a pay-off; every line has momentum. But like life, it's often not clear in the moment quite what the direction is. Go back and watch a season again from beginning to end and the trajectories are startlingly clear. Even moments which appeared entirely aimless are suddenly sodden with purpose. There's constant churning activity – but it's largely happening inside the characters' heads. Everyone in Mad Men hides a secret, often a driving force they're scarcely aware of themselves. They don't know who they are or what they want. Unlike many characters in TV drama, they don't verbally telegraph their motivations: in fact they couldn't if they tried. This is what gives the series such a steady pull: there's a mystery at the core of every character, and they're trying to solve it at the same time as the viewer.

By the time the credits roll in series three you'll be craving season four like a starving bear craves meat. You can gauge how addicted to Mad Men you are by working out how much of your body you'd be prepared to slice off, fry and eat in exchange for a five-minute sneak preview of the next season. I'm currently standing at one little finger, which might not sound like much. But if pushed I could raise it to a thumb. A thumb, goddamit. Mad Men really is that fantastic.

Welcome to Sterling Cooper

On the eve of its UK debut Mad Men creator Matthew Weiner talked about the boozy "house of pain" that his characters work in

JONATHAN BERNSTEIN

As writer and executive producer on the last three seasons of The Sopranos, Matthew Weiner has the blood of Bobby Bacala and Christopher Moltisanti on his hands. His new series, the critically worshipped, Golden Globe-winning Mad Men, is another close study of a secret fraternity where egos clash, tempers flare and bloody vendettas are launched. Mad Men takes place in the Madison Avenue of 1960, when advertising was seen as a sexy, aspirational profession rather than one that needs to be prefaced by an apologetic explanation.

Don Draper, the series' lead character (played by the previously little-known but soon to be big-known Jon Hamm), embodies every attribute that once made advertising guys the envy of the nine-to-five world. He's suave, he's prosperous, he looks good in a suit, he has a bottomless repository of cynical quips, he glides through life in a haze of cigarette smoke, fuelled by martinis and the ministrations of a chic, discrete boho mistress who soothes away the pain of the day before he swans back to the suburbs and his perfect model-pretty wife and high-spirited, unblemished kids.

But Don Draper is an unknowable empty shell, hiding a secret past and utterly detached from his equally at-sea model-pretty wife. And, just as Don has made himself a sexy success by presenting a glossy, smoky facade, so his Manhattan-based agency Sterling Cooper, which made its millions by playing on America's insecurities about all the things they don't have and didn't know they needed, is a barely-hidden house of pain. Women are seen but rarely heard beyond the squeals of pleasure accompanying the regular, friendly slaps on the butt. The mousey girl who shows an aptitude with copy and makes the rare transition from the secretarial pool to the copywriters' desk is regarded with pity and suspicion by all the other females in the office. The only visible black faces are the cleaners who leave in the morning moments before the staff roll in. When a Jewish client comes in for a meeting, a frantic search culls the agency's lone Jew from the mailroom. Sterling Cooper's sole gay employee works overtime presenting himself as a ladies' man and comes close to unravelling when a male client makes a pass at him. The agency boss Roger Sterling (John Slattery, the only nominally recognisable cast member) can't control his raging appetites even after he's felled by a series of heart attacks. And, on the eve of the Kennedy-Nixon election, the pulse-takers of the agency are, almost to a man, convinced of a Nixon victory and confused by the prospect that times may be changing.

For all the secrets and the affairs and the personality clashes and even the physical confrontations, Mad Men unspools at an almost hallucinatory pace. Characters listen and consider what others have said. There are long leisurely moments devoted to people thinking about what has just happened to them. By TV standards – by life standards – Mad Men requires a considerable amount of attention. "Someone was joking with me," says Matthew Weiner. "They said 'you know what your show is? It's the phone's ringing and someone walks into the room but they don't answer it.' I can honestly say that the directorial style and the pace of the show is determined by how I like things. There's so much subterfuge, so much lying and dishonesty when people are together socially, that a lot of what you're seeing when it gets slow is the honesty. Some people have described it as dreamlike but there's always a story being told. I hope that when people watch it they're not doing their chequebooks and talking on the phone because they're going to miss something."

Despite the treatment meted out to anyone who isn't white, male and the right kind of rich – Sterling Cooper's ambitious, privileged twentysomething is an almost universal object of contempt – Weiner is an ardent admirer of the era whose foibles he chronicles: "1960 was just such a fruitful, interesting time in the United States. There was so much intellectual activity going on. There's amazing musical things, amazing books were coming out. Because of the prosperity of the time, people were starting to pay attention to materialism. And also, it really was the apex of New York City. It was the centre of production, publishing, fashion, playwriting, television. It was the biggest port, and then the pill came out in 1960, which was one of the greatest challenges to ever happen to humanity. And at the bottom of all that, advertising was on the verge of a revolution." But when we think of that time in America, our first impressions are the white picket fence and the happy family. "There's such a dichotomy in the culture between the way it's been presented to the world versus the way people were actually living. A lot of the cliched depictions of the 50s – and I picked 1960 as the height of the 50s' [popular US sitcom] Leave It To Beaver and the ideal family with the dad in the hat driving the car – people were laughing at these things back then. We have a perception of the way it was and it's not even close to the way it was."

While fictional advertising men and women are as plentiful now as they were in the days when Rock Hudson and Tony Randall strode the corridors of cinematic agencies, the current incarnation of the copywriter is permanently repenting for the shallowness of their career choice.

Don Draper may be a shadowy figure, unable to fully open himself up to anyone in his life, but he's at his best when he's unashamedly selling, whether it be a product, his agency or his version of himself. "I've always thought that the reason advertising has this appeal is that there's great stock given in jobs that are creative but also make money," says Weiner. "I find that salesmanship is an American religion. It's not about conscience. His conscience should be focused on his life. Business is not about conscience – business is about selling products, which is what he's best at. If you set it now, he would have to be apologising, he would have to be feeling sick about what he does."

As the man behind the suffocation of Christopher Moltisanti and the execution of Bacala in a model train shop, Weiner does not discount the role played by The Sopranos in the ultimate evolution of his subsequent show. "The Mad Men pilot script was how I got my job on The Sopranos. When I got there the show was already a billion dollar success. David (Chase)'s attitude was basically 'serve the story, make sure you're saying something, make everything a little movie'. You start to really think about the audience and surprising them and not giving them what they're expecting. I was there for three seasons, I'd already seen it as a fan for four. It made me raise my game, it made me pay more attention and it made me trust myself."

1960

Season One

EPISODE ONE: Smoke Gets in Your Eyes

**"Mad Men: A term coined in the late 1950s to describe
the advertising executives of Madison Avenue ... they
coined it."**

Welcome to Madison Avenue, March 1960. We begin, as with so
many of director Alan Taylor's shots, with a zoom into the back
of Don Draper's head. Our man is sat in a bar (the Lennox
Lounge in Harlem) scribbling down ideas. The first thing he
does is talk to an elderly, black bus-boy about his cigarettes.
In a world where the maitre d' comes over to check with Draper
that this is all right, we know that for our man in a grey suit,
business is more important than society's mores. While Don sits
and drinks his Old Fashioned cocktail, we pan around the bar
in slo-mo.

At this point, all we can guess is that Don (we don't actually
know his name yet) works in advertising. His girlfriend lives on
57th Street and their acquaintance, it seems, is a casual one: Don
a sharp-suited adman, Midge a modern-looking illustrator. She
makes the extent of their relationship clear: "I don't make plans
and I don't make breakfast."

Meanwhile we're thrust into the world of his office. Sterling
Cooper is populated by twentysomething men with licence to
drink, smoke and harass women. One of the women they hit on
in the lift is Peggy Olson, introduced into the harem by Joan – a
well-proportioned office manager who, seemingly, is the only

one to have the boys under control. Peggy is to be our man Don's new secretary. A shy, dowdily-dressed girl straight out of Miss Deaver's secretarial school. Peggy is led to believe from the other girls that part of her role is as a sexual accessory for her boss – a misreading that ends awkwardly when she places her hand on his. As Peggy says importantly: "I hope you don't think I'm that kind of girl."

Later, however, Pete Campbell, who was frat-boy abhorrent to Peggy when he first met her in Don's corner office, sneaks round to her apartment after his stag do. Peggy (now with contraception courtesy of a flirtatious/judgmental, smoking doctor), seems flattered by his attentions and invites him in as he tells the top of her head: "You must think I'm a creep." Both seem not to know how they should behave – and drunk booty-call sex seems a natural extension of this.

"I'm not going to let a woman talk to me like this." DON

The other key introduction in episode one is Rachel Menken. Rachel, a strong-willed, wealthy, Jewish department-store owner is used by the writers to easily expose Sterling Cooper's misogyny and latent (nearly blatant) difficulty with dealing with a Jewish client. The men in the meeting, including Don's boss, Roger, who drafts in a Jewish chap from the mailroom to make Rachel "comfortable", misread her needs, suggesting cheap coupons – whereas Chanel-wearing Rachel wants to compete with the likes of Macy's. The audacity of her standing up to the men she's giving her money to causes Don to walk out on the meeting. Perhaps he's not the modernist we thought. But as he meets her later for cocktails, he channels his new secretary and implores her to believe that *he* is not that kind of guy.

"Advertising is based on one thing: happiness." DON

Episode one finishes with Don and Pete pitching to the Garners from Lucky Strike. After Don flounders, Pete picks up the Freudian report that Don had put in his bin and tries to promote the deathwish campaign (which, as Chicago ad man Leo Burnett proved with his famous Marlboro County campaign, was actually viable), but the older Garner rejects it out of hand, leaving a furious Don to pick up the pieces – we see his skill at work properly for the first time as he comes up with the slogan "It's toasted", a real slogan which, Mad Men creator Matthew Weiner explains on the DVD commentary, existed pre-1960 but "is a good example of a cold meaningless benefit". It's quite a performance.

So with 45 minutes of nudges to feminism, race inequality, antisemitism, sexual liberation, we leave the smoky world of Sterling Cooper with Don Draper heading back to the street where he lives – not a chic, west-side apartment, but a suburban home in Ossining in upstate New York. Life in Mad Men isn't quite what it seems.

NOTES

- One of the girls in the switchboard was Kristen Schaal, AKA Mel from Flight of the Conchords – which debuted in the US around the same time. She didn't return for a permanent role.

- Along with the back-of-head shots, watch out for some other shots that repeat throughout the series. Including the one from the top of the stairs as Don enters his house.

- Don is snoozing/looking at the trapped fly on the ceiling. There's a big clue there to his state of mind in that shot. But more importantly, watch out for Don's almost teenage levels of sleeping throughout the series too.

- "It's not like there's some magic machine that makes copies of things," ponders Don.

- Lt Donald Francis Draper has a Purple Heart for bravery.

- When Pete shows the picture of his wife, Alison Brie hadn't yet been cast as Trudy. The picture is of Weiner's mother.

20TH CENTURY TALES

- We hear Bert Cooper optimistically mention working on Dick Nixon's famously doomed 1960 election campaign.

- Pete on the burlesque dancer: "Word is she took down more sailors than the Arizona" ie, the American ship sunk by the Japanese at Pearl Harbor.

CULTURE WATCH

- One of Mad Men's most regular cultural comparisons is prompted by scenes shot and lit like a certain realist painter. Mad Men's series creator and executive producer, Matt Weiner, told one of his lighting engineers: "Edward Hopper's going to see this [the lighting] and sue you."

- The instrumental music playing in the burlesque bar on Pete's stag do is Juan Tizol's jazz standard Caravan.

- When the big reveal of Mad Man Don going back to his suburban life in Ossining becomes clear the credits roll out of My Fair Lady's The Street Where You Live. Viewers who have seen beyond this episode might make a Pygmalion connection ...

THOUGHTS FROM THE TYPING POOL

Waifandstray Don is supreme ... powerful and confident, especially in his treatment of Pete. When the Lucky Strike pitch looks like it is going to bomb after his lack of inspiration he pulls the whole situation out of the toilet with a rather shoddy response to Pete's disastrous solution. Pete is "toasted".

It does, however, serve to set up the complicated locking of horns between Don and Pete. Pete has already been dressed down by Don about his treatment of Peggy, despite his own dismissive approach by describing her as "the new girl" to Pete while Peggy was standing by them both. Pete's ambition knows no bounds at this point but he resents the fact that girls in the office are assigned to senior execs as sexual playthings. His lack of social skills and understanding are underlined again in the nightclub when one of the girls that Ken has so easily supplied for the night gives Pete the brush-off.

Nevada As Don is falling asleep on his office sofa and looking at the trapped fly (so absolutely a metaphor for Don and his sense of isolation and exclusion, looking in on life) the light changes and there's a low frequency sound like big guns firing.

JoeDoone Did women really allow themselves to be treated the way Peggy was by Dr Smoker? He's just a moralising perv with a medical certificate. Why did she have to be "examined" in order to be granted the gift of the pill?

Oldmuskrat Yes, the examination did seem unnecessary ... and would only be done (now) if the doctor was looking for a specific gynae problem (to do with infertility) or to do a routine STD swab or smear test. I really don't know what the exam procedures would have been in that early pill era but the doctor doesn't really give her any proper advice apart from the fact that it'll cost her $11 dollars a month (sounds a bit pricey to me ...) and lecture her on the importance of not becoming too promiscuous. Peggy is doing a rather brave and sensible thing here, she wants to become a modern woman.

Sansucre Mad Men/Don Draper owes more than a little from the original Mad Man – Roger Thornhill in North by Northwest, haven't any of you noticed how similar in appearance Jon Hamm is to Cary Grant?

Indeed, from the opening credits, it's obvious that Hitchcock's footprint is all over Mad Men. The graphics are inspired by the opening credits of NBNW and one of Mad Men's main motifs, the image of the back of Don/his silhouette is lifted straight out of Notorious where it serves to remind us that we never know what Devlin is thinking, and used to great effect in Mad Men to illustrate that we will never fully understand or comprehend just who Don Draper is.

Additionally, because Mad Men is filmed using similar filming methods true to the 1960s, ie no hand held cameras, just dolly shots etc, this gives a more detached look, and this, coupled with the tendency for many of the scenes to end with the characters framed by doorways, or the camera drawing away from the shot, serves as a way to remind us that each of the characters are trapped in some way.

EPISODE TWO: Ladies' Room

"Who could not be happy with all this?" DON

Mad Men is littered with key lines that reveal more about the characters than hours of time spent in their company. As Don discusses headshrinkers with Roger after their boozy night of martinis, he utters the above line. As set ups go, it's not a bad one. Who *could* be unhappy?

Ladies' Room, aptly, is our first proper introduction to Don's wife Betty (and Roger's wife Mona) – demonstrating that there's more to this world than these drunken men. Betty doesn't know much about Don's childhood or his worklife. When he's asleep she literally asks him/herself, "who's in there?" He's as much of a mystery to her as he is to the viewers.

There are early signs that things aren't rosy for Betty. Her hands are going numb without any medical symptoms (does she have conversion disorder – a psychiatric illness exhibiting itself in physical form?). Her mother has just died, too. When she crashes her car and is referred to a psychiatrist we see the extent of Don's dominance: he won't let her go, believing (as an ad man might) that happiness equates with consumer contentment: "I always thought people saw psychiatrists when they were unhappy, but I look at you and I look at this and then I think, are you unhappy?"

Eventually, Betty is allowed to see her shrink, although we learn that Don is being tipped off by the doctor. In the sessions Betty echoes Don's bemusement. She's part of the wealthiest generation that has ever lived – "we're all so lucky to be here," she tells the shrink – so why isn't she content?

"You're the new girl, so you might as well enjoy it while it lasts" JOAN HOLLOWAY

New girl Peggy is still learning the ropes. We see her walking past a girl in the toilets crying early on – and the week Peggy has would be enough to bring anyone to tears. First, she's taken for lunch with Ken and the boys where they reveal that there's a sweep on who can sleep with her first. She seems almost flattered until Ken's forceful attempts to get her to take the afternoon off. Then she's taken on a tour of "positively Cro-Magnon" Sterling Cooper by the Ukrainian food-eating charmer Paul Kinsey, who also does a good job of explaining to viewers who does what. Eventually – and after sowing a narrative seed ("you know there *are* women copywriters") – Kinsey too tries to grab her, but we know that she likes slippery Pete and has kept his postcard to the office as a souvenir. After an array of lairy looks and a messed-up bit of typing, Peggy makes to the mirror we saw the girl crying into before – but before she starts, gets hold of herself. As if we didn't know it already, this girl is different.

"Do you belong to someone else?" PAUL KINSEY

Aptly for a show about selling things, much of this episode is about possession, both emotional and material. There's a great deal of talk about what people (particularly women) want, and not what they need. We get the hint from the conversation about nannies that Don isn't from the same class as the others, and his lack of possessions as a kid perhaps explains why he endows them with so much power. Like the fridge, car and house in the suburbs, Betty appears to be another one of his possessions. And his approach to fixing her unhappiness? A new gold watch. Paul, meanwhile, presumes that Peggy also belongs to Don. The only person so far who doesn't seem to be defined by what she has is Midge – who throws her new TV out of the window. "I live in the moment, nothing is everything," she tells Don. Independent and free, she seems the polar opposite to nervous Betty.

NOTES

- Peggy is from – traditionally Norwegian – Bay Ridge, Brooklyn.

- Line of the episode comes from Ken: "So Pegs, are you part of our nation's military industrial boyfriend-girlfriend complex?"

- Betty focuses on the construct too – she worries that, God forbid: "Sally could have survived and gone on living with a scar on her face."

- Sally Draper gets told off for having a plastic bag over her head … not for fear of suffocation but in case she'd thrown its contents on the floor.

20TH CENTURY TALES

- Roger notes that his parents got rid of a German nanny "after the Lindbergh baby".

- The firm is pitching for Nixon's campaign; Don (who seems relecuctant to get political) says Dicky already has a man – former producer on The Lone Ranger turned political imagemaker, Ted Rogers.

- The Right Guard aerosol deodorant ad is the first major reference to the space race and the Cold War. And their interconnectedness – as Don says of potential consumers: "They see a rocket, they start building a bomb shelter."

CULTURE WATCH

- Midge has been using her new TV to watch comedy stunt show People Are Funny. We see Bob and Sally watching it later, as well as Shirley Temple's Storybook.

- While Peggy is typing and being leered at the song playing is I Can Dream Can't I? by the Andrews Sisters. She can.

- Midge has a touch of the Holly Golightlys about her. She leaves Don to go to a party and "act surprised when Jack Kerouac doesn't show". Not to mention preempting Keith Moon by lobbing her TV out of the window.

- Kinsey derides Pete to Peggy with a Twilight Zone quote: "A man who recently discovered that the only place for his hand is in your pocket." Oops!

- Roger's 16-year-old won't get out of bed. One of the character's son's inability to get out of bed is a major part of a key Mad Men book, John Cheever's Bullet Park.

- Some distinctly non-period music, the Cardigans' Great Divide, plays over the credits. It begins: "There's a monster growing in our heads…"

THOUGHTS FROM THE TYPING POOL

Nevada Midge is such a contrast to all the other women we've met so far. When Don mentions Betty, Midge says "Don't talk to me about her …" and we might expect her to go on to say she feels jealous or upset as the mistress, but she says "it makes me feel cruel". Almost as though Betty is a child.

Oldmuskrat On first viewing I thought the writers were dropping a hint here that Betty might eventually have a serious nervous breakdown (as in Plath's The Bell Jar for instance) or that the hands thing might be an early sign of MS.

Noseyrosie Also Betty's psychological distress manifesting itself in physical symptoms is similar to Tony Soprano [on which Weiner was a key writer]. He reluctantly went to a shrink after his own physical symptoms (sudden blackouts) were suspected to have psychological roots.

Bluewillow The restaurant featuring steak tartare is 21, the ultimate WASP power restaurant where Roger and Don are flexing their expense accounts ... with Mona making her debut (played by John Slattery's real wife Talia Balsam). Also Don looks like the man in Chesterfield cigarette ads – great referencing of American adverts.

EPISODE THREE: Marriage Of Figaro

"Draper? Who knows anything about that guy? No one's ever lifted that rock. He could be Batman for all we know." HARRY CRANE

This episode contains the first hints that all is not as it should be with Donald Draper. First, he's greeted on the train by an old army chum who calls him "Dick Whitman". Then, after his daughter Sally's birthday party – during which he drinks half a bottle of whisky and half a fridge of beer – he disappears. We find him sitting – possibly suicidally – in front of a level crossing before returning home, as if nothing happened, with a new family dog.

Draper spent the previous day with department store heiress Rachel Menken at her shop, working out a new business plan. Consultancy research into rivals like Sak's, Henri Bendel and Bonwit Teller proved that none of the Sterling Cooper staff have actually visited Menken's so Don sets about righting this wrong. His flirtation with Rachel grows and she even gives him some medieval knight cufflinks (you can't see under *his* armour) before they kiss on the roof of the building against a beautifully shot New York cityscape before Rachel reveals that her mother died in childbirth and Don tells her he's married. Scared off, she asks him: "What do you do? Just kiss women all the time, women you're not married to?" Er ...

Back in Ossining the next day, Don wrestles with a flat-pack playhouse in front of a drooling Francine while Betty prepares for Sally's party, to which all their friends and local divorcee Helen Bishop are invited. When everyone arrives Don is sent to capture proceedings on his home movie camera. Draper seems like an outsider at his own party, capturing private moments from behind his lens. Once he's behind this fourth wall, he never seems to return.

The women's focus, though, is on Helen. They cattily question her fondness for walking (walking!), and ask where she went on her honeymoon (Paris, actually). Helen's having none of it (nor Carlton's offer to "throw a ball around" with her son), she doesn't need their approval and such is her confidence (she's a Volkswagen driver) that when she's sat with fellow outsider Don, Betty is swift to shoo him away. Eventually though, it's the woman with the frozen cake in her freezer who saves the day after Don goes MIA.

"There's going to be dinner waiting for me when I get home." PETE

While Don is running away from his wife, Pete is running home to his new one. After returning to the office to find a Chinese family using it to do dry cleaning, he's coy with the details of his honeymoon (Ken describes his tales as very "Ladies Home Journal"). This is the first time we get to see a human side of Pete: he's almost apologetic to Peggy for their tryst ("I'm married now," he tells her – as if it was all right before) and keen to get home to his wife while the rest of the crew run off to Lansky's bar. Like Peggy, he's learning to play a role but doesn't quite know what that role is – frequently saying the wrong thing, like suggesting dinner with Don and Betty after Don half-heartedly mentions looking forward to meeting Trudy.

Pete is also the only one open to – or at least willing to admit to – liking the Volkswagen ad, even in the face of Roger and Don's dismissiveness. He might be an entitled, rude, sex pest but he's as confused as anyone.

NOTES

- Don is necking tins of Fielding Beer, which didn't exist at the time, a rare inaccuracy.

- Carlton and Francine's son Ernie gets a slap from one of the other men. Carlton's intervention is to ask "do you want some more?" before sending him to "get your mother to clean this up".

- The casual antisemitism continues with Francine's views on Boca Raton's mosquitoes/Florida's Jewish population: "Those won't be the only long noses."

- Betty graduated from Bryn Mawr College in 1954 before heading to Italy.

20TH CENTURY TALES

- We open with one of the most famous ads of the century, VW's counterintuitive Lemon ads from Doyle Dane Bernbach, which changed the face of advertising. The conservatism of Sterling Cooper's men indicates where they stand in the current market – other young firms like DDB and (later) Mary Wells were innovating but Don complains: "You can hardly see the product."

- The boys talk about France getting the bomb in the lift – probably with regard to French weapons testing in the Sahara, which started in February 1960. There's a nod to American arrogance: "There's no ways the Frogs came up with it on their own," which conveniently ignores European scientists' involvement in the development of nuclear weapons.

- Before Don retunes the radio to the classical station, a newsreader is discussing a tax evasion trial in New York. It doesn't name anyone but it's likely that this is a reference to Johnny Dioguardi, a Jimmy Hoffa acolyte and mafiosa.

CULTURE WATCH

- The girls are passing around the recently legalised Lady Chatterley's Lover. Peggy is keen to experience "the desperate passion of the forbidden".

- Pete dismissively refers to Rachel as "Molly Goldberg" – the matriarch from comedy/soap radio and TV show The Goldbergs which was about a Jewish family from the Bronx.

- Betty was in Italy "right around the time" of Jean Negulesco's Three Coins In The Fountain, the story of three American girls looking for love in Rome.

- Betty rolls her eyes at the new dog over Bobby Vinton's version of PS I Love You. (Not the Beatles' version, which was a McCartney original).

THOUGHTS FROM THE TYPING POOL

JoeDoone Does Don buy Sally a dog because of the association with Rachel's security canines? Surely yes.

Jreid Regarding (the episode's title) The Marriage of Figaro – the opera is all about marriage (unsurprisingly!) in its various incarnations – Figaro and Susanna the happy couple about to tie the knot but continuously interrupted by the schemers around them. It features an unhappy marriage between the Count and Countess – the Countess has two very famous arias about her philandering husband who she loves despite his continuous betrayals ... does that sound like Betty? Having said that, Figaro is the manservant continuously outsmarting his wealthy masters, which does make me think of Don, given his background.

Bashal Voi Che Sapete was playing when Helen arrived. The singer, Cherubino, is a trouser role (a girl playing a boy). This may have been a reference to Helen arriving in slacks, rather than the flouncy frocks of all the other women. The aria asks the question, "You ladies who know all about love, is that what I'm feeling?"

Nevada I loved the disturbance Helen Bishop creates in that oh-so-tidy world. I also noticed she was the only woman in trousers (capri pants?). While the other women fear and therefore despise her, she is the modern one, doing fine by her independent self. The men are just ghastly, so cock-sure with so little to be sure about. What a fragile society it is to be so easily destabilised by one woman. She's almost back from the future, so out of place is she to them.

EPISODE FOUR: New Amsterdam

"We gave you everything, we gave you your name. And what have you done with it?" ANDREW CAMPBELL

Despite being filmed in California, Mad Men is one of the most NYC of New York City shows. Never more so than in New Amsterdam, which weaves threads between Pete's rich Manhattan history, the new money of the Vogels (Trudy's parents – her father is a salesman-done-good at Lux Chemical), Don's misunderstanding of how the "marvellous machine" of class works and the Bethlehem Steel campaign.

Let's focus on Pete. Here we witness his struggle to maintain an equilibrium between the three roles in his life. That of son to New York social royalty – to whom his career is "no job for a white man", his role as husband to Trudy and son-in-law to her generous, parvenu parents, who inadvertently emasculate him when stumping up for the marital home, and finally, his role as a subordinate to Don.

You could argue that Pete's trying to do the right thing by each and ends up being eaten up by his neuroses. He is (and probably knows he is) employed on the basis of his name, despite being talented. But while Trudy's mother revels in dropping his family's name to the head of the condo board, Pete is reluctant to use it. It's both a gift – as his father believes – and a curse. How can he be his own man when Don, father-in-law Tom and his father won't let him? "I came to this place and you people tell me that I'm good with people. Which is strange, because I'd never heard that before," he tells Don, exasperated. But Pete doesn't appreciate what he's got either: he tells others "you always get what you want". He can't see the city for the skycrapers.

Pete begrudgingly looks up to Don as a father figure – but he only antagonises Draper by publicly taking the side of Walter from Bethlehem Steel, and then pitching his (better) Backbone Of America idea to the client during a hotel rendezvous with some cocktails and escorts. Walter then drops Pete in it while Don is pitching his O! Little Town idea; a breakdown in command that leads to Don demanding his sacking. Pete is only saved by – what else? – his name. "You're going to need a stronger stomach if you're going to be back in the kitchen seeing how the sausage is made," Bert tells Don as he explains why a member of the Dychman dynasty is inexpendable.

"Honestly, I think she's jealous of me. I've seen it before, I was in a sorority." BETTY

Pete's turmoil often runs in parallel with that of Betty. She, like Pete, wants to be appreciated. With a husband who spends his spare time sketching ads, it takes the attentions of a young boy to put a smile on her face. Having agreed to babysit for Helen Bishop, Betty finds herself in the bizarre situation of telling off Helen's son Glen for walking in and staring at her while she's on the toilet. After apologising, he tells her "your hair is so beautiful, you look like a princess" before asking for a lock of it, which Betty, surprised and a little flattered, gives him.

It's easy to draw a line between her shrink comparing her to a little girl and Betty enjoying the company of a little boy. But really, as she says to the doctor about Glen not getting any attention, she has the same problem. Glen's reaction is to act out inappropriately, hers is a nervous one. For those wondering what could have inspired the writers to create such an odd moment – the incident was inspired by something Matthew Weiner did himself as a kid.

Finally – she projects her own anxieties onto Helen – telling her shrink that Helen is jealous and worrying for Glen: "That poor little boy. The person taking care of him isn't giving him what he needs."

NOTES

- Pete and Trudy's place costs $30,000, about $220,000 in 2010. They're at 83rd and Park in the Upper East Side.

- The Dychman family that Pete comes from is real – they came to New Amsterdam in the 1600s and owned most of Harlem. "His grandfather dropped the lot in 1929, panicked. Some people have no confidence," laments Bert.

- Glen Bishop is played by Marten Weiner who is, of course, Matthew's son.

- Bert Cooper worries about seeing Pete's mother at old money summer resort Fishers Island – where Ike Eisenhower himself was known to golf.

- One has to admire Pete's boast, "Direct marketing, I thought of that! Turns out it already existed but I arrived at it independently."

20TH CENTURY TALES

- Helen is off stuffing envelopes for JFK. The leaflet she brings back appears to be a mixture of original JFK paraphernalia Photoshopped by the Mad Men production team.

- "The Armory, when are they going to tear that dinosaur down?" asks Trudy of the beautiful Seventh Regiment Armory on Park Avenue.

- Sal's artwork is compared to the boldly graphic art deco WPA ads. The WPA was one of Roosevelt's New Deal agencies.

- "Sterling Cooper has more failed artists and intellectuals than the Third Reich," says Don.

CULTURE WATCH

- We open on Pete and the boys listening to the Billboard-topping live comedy album The Button-Down Mind Of Bob Newhart. "It's not Lenny Bruce," sighs Kinsey.

- Pete offers to get Walter tickets to Bye, Bye Birdie on Broadway.

- It's interesting to see Bethlehem Steel mentioned while at its postwar peak (1960 was the first year US steel imports exceeded exports). If we zip forward 45 years to The Wire, we see the result of its demise in the desolation of the Baltimore docks.

- Glen has to go to bed before dirt farm sitcom The Real McCoys.

- Tom Vogel refers to two Lux ads starring Natalie Wood and Janet Leigh.

- Betty is reading to Bobby and Sally from Nursery Friends From France (1950) by Olive Beaupre Miller. Miller's company The Bookhouse For Children was a pioneering one which employed almost solely women.

- Pete looks over New York and the title credits to Ella Fitzgerald singing Manhattan. "We'll settle down, right here in town."

THOUGHTS FROM THE TYPING POOL

Oldmuskrat Pete can't seem to please anyone. His father looks down on his advertising job (not a gentleman's option like law) and Campbell Snr is piling on the burden of the family's heritage "we gave you your name..." etc while sitting there in his shorts! It is actually Pete's mother who has the grand lineage though, Pete's dad just married into it ... what a snob.

JoeDoone After Pete's sacking is reversed, Don and Roger have a drink, and their very different outlooks on life emerge. Roger tells Don that Don's generation don't know how to drink properly, that they're eaten up with "imaginary wounds." Don retorts with "Maybe I'm not as happy being powerless as you are."

Nevada I enjoy the Japanese thing that Bert has going on. I get the impression that he sits up there in his office, like a god on Mt Olympus, coming down to keep the mortals in order. Making them take their shoes off is a nice Japanese custom but it's also a powerplay, putting the power very much with Bert and discomfiting his visitors. Considering the feelings of many Americans towards Japan in 1960 (VJ Day is still today recognised in Rhode Island), Bert's connection puts him outside the norm. Perhaps he has a Japanese past from pre-WW2?

Wanchai The screen, lamp and side table are Chinese not Japanese. I think he was aiming for an Asian rather than Japanese vibe, Chinoiserie was old money chic in the fifties and sixties, Norman Parkinson used it in his fashion shoots. It also goes well with the Rothko (that Bert buys in series two). I think the room is saying more about where Bert wishes to position himself socially, with the old money connoisseurs, than his history.

Meet the cast

JON HAMM (DON DRAPER)
the man in the grey flannel suit...

CHRISSY ILEY

There are many things to love about Mad Men. Its impeccable style – the suits, the martinis, the ashtrays. The lighting (fluorescent office, amber nightclub), the permanent halo of smoke, the way women wear corsetry to work and are revered and despised in equal parts, the sexualised selling of ideas – all are period-perfect. It's a Polaroid of the advertising world of early sixties Manhattan on Madison Avenue. It is politically incorrect and recreates an era where great change was about to happen but had not happened yet. It has the repression of the Fifties more than the swing of the Sixties. At the heart of the drama is Don Draper, rarely without a chunky glass of bourbon in one hand and a cigarette in the other. He has a Grace Kelly-style wife, a beatnik mistress and another lover, a gorgeous Jewish woman from the Upper East Side.

Draper is played by Jon Hamm. This year, he won the Golden Globe for best actor ahead of Hugh Laurie (House) and Jonathan Rhys Meyers (The Tudors). He is 37 and is being compared with George Clooney, who was about that age when he got his ER break and had similarly been toiling unnoticed in lesser-known US series.

I am waiting for Hamm in a cafe in Silver Lake, a boho-chic part of LA, wondering what he is going to look like without the suit and Brylcreemed hair. And here he is, as tall, lean and buff as could be in jeans, battered navy polo shirt, all unshaven and solicitous. How is my jetlag? How is my life? He recommends Devil's Nest, a scramble of avocado, sour cream, spicy sausage.

Hamm is not self-consciously Hollywood, showy or full of himself, which probably comes from several years working at the coalface of showbusiness and before that as a waiter and a teacher. "I taught daycare when I was in college. I taught after-school stuff for little kids.

"I was a theatre major in college and they didn't prepare you for the massive amount of rejection you have to go through. Most people who are successful, like George Clooney and Brad Pitt, had to eat shit at a lot of auditions and still not get the parts. So you have to develop resilience. Especially for Mad Men, where it took seven auditions to get the part. People really needed convincing that they wanted me."

Matthew Weiner pushed for Hamm despite the cable network's nervousness that, as this was the cable channel AMC's first foray into drama series, it needed the security of a star name.

Hamm had been a regular for three years on a show called The Division. "It was on a network called Lifetime, which is soft programming for women. It was a cop show, five women and me, but the women got to be much more macho than me. I was the slightly emasculated cop; now I get to be a little more masculine," he says. But, he shrugs, he's no alpha male. "I was raised by a single mother and I've been in a 10-year relationship with my girlfriend. My whole life I've been surrounded by women."

Does he at all resemble the slick but haunted ad man Don Draper? "The closest thing I have in common with Don is that I'm looking for something. If you look at the literature of the early sixties, like Cheever and Updike, it's existentialist. People sitting around smoking, thinking 'what am I doing with my life?'. Postwar America was riding as high as it's ever ridden. It had an incredibly paternalistic sense of its place in the world. America was the good cop. It healed Japan after it had utterly destroyed it, protected the world from communism. Americans had money, ability to travel and see the world. And at the core of it was: I'm still not happy. What Don Draper is doing is trying to sell happiness because he can't buy it himself. I think that resonates."

The eggs arrive and he eats heartily. Does he smoke as much as Draper? "I gave up 10 years ago when I started teaching kids. I don't miss the hacking cough in the morning or the mouth that tastes like cat litter, but I miss it when I'm on this show. It's glamorous, I got to tell you. [They smoke a non-nicotine herbal blend.] In the show, we know smoking kills, but we don't give a shit. These guys had three-martini lunches ... I appreciate alcohol. I love the place that alcohol holds in our society, but I'd never attempt to drink as much as Draper."

Hamm may relate to the smoking and the drinking, but not to the way the women are treated. He is devoted to his girlfriend, the actress and writer Jennifer Westfeldt, while Draper and his colleagues spend most of their time humiliating women when they are not sleeping with them and even when they are. They refer to Peggy, his frumpy secretary, as "a lobster. All the meat in the tail". At one point, Draper says to one of his inamoratas: "What you call love was invented by guys like me to sell nylons."

Draper sells lies for a living. He cheats. He is emotionally withholding, morally ambiguous, with a past he can't face up to, yet we can't help rooting for him. There's a genius in this portrayal. Hamm stares into his Devil's Nest. "There's a vicarious thrill in it. When we see people misbehave, sometimes we want them to get away with it.

"I've gotten away with a lot in my life. The older you get the more you realise you're not getting away with it, it's taking its toll somewhere. So you try not to put yourself in those situations. Part of the mysterious process called growing up. Some people do that better than others. It's a daily struggle, especially in this city where everyone is a child and often rewarded for it."

I tell him I cannot imagine him as a child. "Well, I was forced to grow up very early because I lost my mother when I was 10. So that tends to take a lot of childhood out of the equation and you become very aware of adult things."

Hamm's parents divorced when he was two and he lived with his mother. "She died suddenly over the course of about three months. A stomach ache one day turned out to be an advanced cancer that spread rapidly through her internal organs. She had two-thirds of her colon removed and it killed her.

"When you are 10, you just don't have the tools to process it. You're coming home from playing kick-ball to talks about how they've got to set you up a trust fund [which paid for his high-school education]. I do have very good memories of being a kid running around, but that all pretty much got lost. It was hard to bounce back from losing my mum. It's an incredibly tough process and you see a lot of that in Don as well. His childhood was … " He searches for the word. Tortured? "Yeah." This would be the moment where Don Draper would light a cigarette and smoke the pain away. Hamm dips his sourdough into his eggs and swills it about.

It must have been strange suddenly to go and live with his father? "Sort of. Though I loved my dad and I would see him every other weekend. It wasn't like he was a guy I didn't know. He had not remarried, but he had two children from a previous marriage, one of whom was living with him, as well as my 80-year-old grandmother.

"My dad was in many ways essentially Don Draper. A businessman in the Sixties, very powerful, self-assured. I didn't find out about that when I was a kid. He passed away when I was 20. We didn't have a chance for many adult discussions or to deal with each other as adults. He was sick for several years. He just degenerated over the last couple of years until he passed away. He packed a lot into his 63 years. It was a hard life."

Hamm came west to LA from St Louis in 1995, prepared for hard work. "I tried to get my affairs in St Louis in order the last year I was there, but I was never very good with money and by the end of the summer I had saved only $150. Fortunately, gas was cheaper then and I made it here in my car. The car died an interesting death. I had $1,600 of parking tickets accrued in my first four or five years here and the good people of Los Angeles decided to take the car back on their own."

In Los Angeles he lived in a big house, just down the road from where we are having breakfast, with four other guys. In those days, the eastern district of Silver Lake was not cool or sought-after. It was rough. "It was a crazy house and it was so cheap even I could afford it. An 85-year-old woman owned the house. She was a soap actress who lived in New York and we were four guys, my size and bigger. But we broke so many pieces of furniture, these little-old-lady chairs you would sit on and they would crack. Plus we would have parties and the keg would leak. It was my job as the diplomat of the group to say to her, 'Marilyn, we love you' and make her feel good. I was always the one who was behind on the rent. I was very proud that once I started working I was able to pay her back completely."

Hamm now lives just down the road in his own place with his girlfriend. "We met through some mutual friends at somebody's birthday party. We didn't really hit it off immediately. She thought I was a cocky asshole."

Soon after, she called him from New York to ask if he would come over and work on a project with her. It started off as a sketch. She thought maybe it would be a play and it turned into the critically acclaimed movie Kissing Jessica Stein in 2001. "I was working downtown as a set dresser for some very bad softcore porn when I got the call from New York. I was making $150 a day and my friend was the electrician, so we would share a ride to work. I would carry my little bucket around and move what needed to be moved, but I would be terrible at it. I would fall asleep in a corner and they could never find me. So when I got the call, even though we had not particularly hit it off, I was like, yes, anything but this. I had no money, no car and all these parking tickets. Anything to get out of here.

"I borrowed the money from a friend and went to New York and we did this cool little play which turned into Kissing Jessica Stein. That's when Jen and I became really close. A year after that, we started going out and that was 10 years ago. We just had our anniversary in Mexico. We had a blast. We very much complement each other in this insane industry. We live and we work it out together. It's been great."

It sounds as if she was a grounding force in his life? "It's hard when you move cities and don't have a lot of friends and you're just trying to keep your head above water and trying not to get caught up in all this bullshit, to go out on auditions and not be totally soul-crushed when you don't get it. Especially out here, especially in the television industry where they dangle all this in front of you…

"And then they pull it back at the last second every time. How many more times am I going to be like Charlie Brown trying to kick the football and have them pull it away again? A lot of people after five or six times think, this is not for me, I'm done. It is so arbitrary and capricious.

"Eventually I got there. Everybody on Mad Men is at the top of their game and it feels great." And is he happy? "Absolutely I am. I have a pretty stable relationship that brings me love and happiness and comfort. I have a great house and a great dog." He shows me a picture of a dog wearing a baseball cap.

What about babies? "I don't necessarily want kids. A lot of

our friends are having children and I don't know if it's for me. I haven't come down hardcore on either side of the argument. I think when people come from a stable family having children becomes a celebration and I'm not sure it would be that way for me."

And perhaps, for the moment, being the main guy in the best show on TV is enough. "It doesn't suck," he admits.

With that, he picks up the bill for breakfast as if that's perfectly normal when, in fact, it's unheard of.

No Hollywood actor has even bought me a chai latte before. And then he offers to drive me home, as he doesn't want me to wait and call a taxi. I live half an hour away. We sit in his car listening to Steve Jones on the radio. How much better can it be?

EPISODE FIVE: 5G

"Who is Donald Draper?" ADAM WHITMAN

Sterling Cooper's major campaign in 5G is for Liberty Savings Capital. The team come up with a way to rebrand bank accounts so that men who don't want their wives to see where some of their cash is going can have statements sent to their office. And the man who dreams up the name "Liberty Capital Executive Account"? A man who could clearly use that service – one Donald Draper.

Draper's life is, according to Midge, "in a million pieces". She sees that the man she is sleeping with is different from the man in the grey suit at Sterling Cooper: "You come in here, acting like somebody else," she tells him. That there are two sides to Don is never clearer than when someone from his darkest past emerges out of nowhere.

We knew something was odd when, in Marriage Of Figaro, Don's army buddy on the train referred to him as "Dick Whitman" – so when Peggy interrupts an important meeting to tell him that an Adam Whitman is waiting for him, the intrigue grows. Adam has seen Don's award picture in the paper and sought him out: "It's you, it's really you, Dick," the man says to a shaken, denying, Don who sends him away coldly before meeting him later at a cafe.

Why is Don so cold to a man who appears to be a close relation? It becomes clear that Don – who was apparently once Dick – left Adam and his now dead family members at some point and reinvented himself as "Don Draper". There are hints of a dreary early life, and some complicated relationships: when Adam's mother is mentioned Don says: "She wasn't my mother. She never let me forget that." We get no further clarification – Don/Dick tells Adam that their reunion "never happened" before heading back to the office where Betty and the kids (and a terrified Peggy who thinks Don was with his mistress) are waiting for the Draper family photo.

That other family photo – the picture of a young Dick and Adam Whitman together – is burned by Don, who later contacts Adam in his bleak hotel room. Don tries to make Adam go away, offering him the 5G bonus that he's been keeping in a drawer at home. Someone get that man an Executive Account! Adam, who is clearly still in awe of Dick/Don ("You look more like you now – the eyes, the stubble …") is heartbroken, rather than thrilled, by the payoff. As far as Don is concerned, the threat of losing his new life is more important than losing his last tie to his own family. "I have too much here," he warns. He's a paper construct that Adam's appearance threatens to hold a flame underneath.

"Who the hell is Ken Cosgrove? He's from Burlington, Vermont. His father is a salesman." PETE

This episode's major subplot is one of this series' best. As Don is being praised from all and sundry for his Ad Age award, account man Ken is getting patted on the back too. His short story, Tapping A Maple On A Cold Vermont Morning, has been published in The Atlantic Monthly. Don and Roger – who have bigger things to concern themselves with than writing fiction – are both impressed, which makes Pete and creative man Paul's jealously only intensify. "It's a national magazine," Campbell whimpers, while Kinsey can only damn him with the faint praise of "they (his stories) don't even sound stupid." Kinsey's assertions that his so-far mythical novels are unimaginably good are made comic by the fact that we know he'll never write them.

Ken's achievement serves only to show further how Pete is devoured by the achievements of others. How dare a salesman's son get published before him? How dare Draper tell him what to do? And so he pressures his wife Trudy into meeting an old flame (her "first" she reminds Pete) to see what strings she can pull to get his own short story published. Charlie, the publishing agent, only wants to pull the strings of her pants, though. When he is rebuffed, he gets Pete a slot in the Boy Scouts' Boy's Life magazine for $40 (Ken got $100). The major character reveal is that Pete, who last episode was beginning to show a more human side, seems perfectly willing for Trudy to sleep with Charlie if it means a slot in the New Yorker for him.

Either way, the last laugh goes to Cosgrove after Kinsey apologises for his less-than-magnanimous barbs (ie ripping the article up in front of the office girls) by saying "I didn't realise I was competing with you too." "You lost," replies Ken.

NOTES

- Adam works as a janitor at "American Calculator in the Empire State Building."
- Betty thinks her perfectly normal-sized daughter Sally "looks fat in their family portrait."

CULTURE WATCH

- When Midge gives a fake name on the phone to Peggy she uses boozy jazz musician trumpeter Bix Beiderbecke's.
- Other ad men-turned-writers include Salman Rushdie, Peter Carey, F Scott Fitzgerald, Joseph Heller (who also got his first short published in the Atlantic), Fay Weldon and Elmore Leonard.

THOUGHTS FROM THE TYPING POOL

Nevada The scenes between Don and Adam were moving to watch. Don's break with his past is a Faustian pact and this is a moment where we see the price he pays – both in terms of his fear of being discovered and the loss of his little brother.

JoeDoone Any time I get within shouting distance of liking Pete, he shouts back that I'm an idiot. He is born into success and can't understand the notion of someone succeeding on merit, whereas Bert made himself successful and Don is very much his own creation. Pete deeply resents the fact that Ken has done so well because Ken has done it entirely on his own merits and without connections, whereas Pete has been born into success and is only too ready to use each and every connection to advance himself.

ArundelXVI Betty says "It's like I'm speaking a foreign language" (when she visits the office). A book called Voltaire's Bastards by Canadian essayist John Ralston Saul spends a lot of time describing "Courtesans of Power" in a look at the corporate world.

The Betty quote reminds me of his descriptions of how corporate courtesans hijack language for their own ends with horrible things described as great opportunities in that world. Purposefully meant to be unknowable to an outsider, like a baffled Betty.

Mad Men often reminds me of this book, I wonder if Weiner read it. One thing Saul describes rather acidly is how CEOs of massive corporations present themselves as hard-working, tireless innovators. When they show no such wear and tear at all: these rational courtesans of power are inheritors. They did not invent or build the companies, they slickly positioned themselves to reach that top spot.

In contrast, Saul describes the actual creators – the dreamers, the eccentrics, the wildcatters who actually did create these companies – as visionaries who are damaged as humans in some way, rough and ragged. Both Bert Cooper and Conrad Hilton [Hilton appears in series three] seem that way to me on the show, driven eccentrics who created something out of nothing. But depend on a corporate courtier class to keep it going, knowing that whomever suceeds them will seize the crown and claim he earned it on his own.

Oldmuskrat Ties in with Bert's Japonisme fad. Japanese society is the epitome of that classic conservative rather inward-looking feudal mentality where family connections are important in business and the notion of change is difficult to comprehend. This is reflected in the way Cooper as the senior partner likes to run things. There is a strict pecking order and junior executives (like Pete) are carpeted if they step out of line and suggest new ideas.

DellaMirandola It's only when Don sits down with Adam in the coffee shop that we finally have confirmation that he really is Dick Whitman. I do find Don unbelievably and inexcusably heartless here. Since nobody really knows anything about his past, it wouldn't be impossible for him to find a way to keep some kind of contact with Adam and explain him away to anyone if necessary. It's Don's own decision to cut him off with a big fat bribe.

EPISODE SIX: Babylon

"Jews have lived in exile for a long time and managed to make a go of it. Maybe it has something to do with the fact that we thrive at doing business with people who hate us." RACHEL MENKEN

Mad Men's tackling of huge subjects within the framework of Sterling Cooper is key to the show's purpose of exploring the 20th century. We've seen that casual antisemitism is rife in New York's offices and suburbs but Judaism and the young state of Israel become prominent here in Babylon.

First, we meet a team from Israeli tourism and Olympic Cruise Lines who wish to market the Israeli riviera: "We'd like to think that if Beirut is the Paris of the Middle East, Haifa can be the Rome," Lily Meyer tells them. They've already visited DDB's Bill Bernbach but found his ideas kitsch and fancy trying the more "traditional" (ouch!) Sterling Cooper.

There are nods towards the USA's intertwined postwar history with Israel – "America has a love affair with Israel," says Meyer – but while the government has a vested interest in the safety of the new state, the waspy inhabitants of Sterling Cooper still see Jews as "others".

Pete (who's been at the Freud again) suggests a holiday to a dangerous place might be thrilling and is, as usual, ignored before getting peeved at the notion of "positively Soviet" kibbutzes. "The only thing this place has going for it? The people are good-looking," they decide. Which leads Don neatly to Rachel Menken.

"I'm the only Jew you know in New York?" she asks him when they meet at the Pierre. Rachel helps Don visualise Israel in ad terms: "It's more an idea than a place." Don, more an idea than a person, still appeals to Menken, who later rings her sister to say she's met a man, preferring to imply he's a drunk rather than a gentile. "Sometimes good things come but there's no future in them," she muses.

Don later nips to Midge's to be interrupted by another man – lank-haired co-op theatre man Roy, the Kerouac to Don's Sloane Wilson – who judges 5.31-train-catching, company man Don immediately, and constantly challenges him. "How do you sleep?" he asks. "On a bed of money," replies Don. Touché. You can see the cultural tectonic plates rubbing together.

"We both know I'll find a more permanent situation and you'll find a new model. The 61s are coming out soon."
JOAN

After we meet Roger's mardy daughter Margaret, there's a reveal with a post-coital Roger sat on his bed moaning to someone out of shot about "what we did wrong". It's not his wife there, but Joan. Their affair has lasted a year and seems to be a mutually beneficial arrangement. Roger loves the "sneaking around", while Joan is quite happy seeing other men and partying. But such is Roger's desire to have her for himself he buys her a bird so if she has her own apartment she won't flutter away while Roger isn't there.

"I don't think anyone wants to be one of a hundred colours in a box." PEGGY

Kinsey had previously sown the seed for Peggy to move up within Sterling Cooper. Here, she takes her chance as during a lipstick brainstorm with the other girls Peggy idly referred to a bin of tissues covered in lipstick as a "basket of kisses". Freddie might be a "schicker" but he can see talent. Even if he describes Peggy's breakthrough as "like watching a dog playing the piano". As Joan tells Peggy that Freddie wants her to write some copy she's half-proud, half-jealous. Would Joan rather be doing that than wiggling her backside through the one-way glass of the market research room?

NOTES

- We flash back to Don's youth for the first time when he falls down the stairs – and witnesses the birth of his half-brother, Adam.

- "To think one of the great beauties, and there she is, so old. I'd just like to disappear at that point." Betty shows her fear of ugliness and decay again when talking about Joan Crawford.

- Was Roger deliberately getting the Jewish names wrong? He mispronounces the chap from the tourist board's name before saying: "Tel-Avenue is about to have a Hilton."

- Betty nods back to her Bryn Mawr days when she quotes an Introduction to Basic Anthropology while discussing Michaelangelo and the pygmies. Rachel, we learn, went to Barnard College.

- More Roger gold: "We've got oysters Rockefeller, beef Wellington, Napoleons … we leave this lunch alone it'll take over Europe."

20TH CENTURY TALES

- The Rosenbergs – the American communist couple who were controversially executed in 1953 for espionage – are a repeated MM reference. Here, Sal dismisses a Belle Jolie lipstick for being "Ethel Rosenberg pink". Betty's first kiss was with a boy called Rosenberg, incidentally.

- Rachel reminds Don that Adolf Eichmann has just been captured. Making this episode set around May 1960.

- Joan drops some McLuhan to Peggy: "You know what they say, the medium is the message."

CULTURE WATCH

- "Did you just get a library card?" asks Betty. Babylon is full of books. We see Don reading Betty's copy of The Best Of Everything by Rona Jaffe. "It's better than the Hollywood version" which starred Joan Crawford. "Salvatore couldn't stop talking about her," says Don of the actress/gay icon.

- The popularity of Leon Uris's novel Exodus, is central to the Israeli plot. "Soon to be a major motion picture starring Paul Newman," says Lily Meyer proudly.

- When Rachel tells Roy that Don is an ad man, she says: "We've all got to serve somebody." Did a fledgling young Village singer by the name of Zimmerman overhear her?

- Roy's friend Ian plays Babylon, a version of Psalm 137 as arranged by Don McLean on 1971's American Pie LP. The man playing box harp is Mad Men composer David Carbonara.

THOUGHTS FROM THE TYPING POOL

Nevada As Don watches his young self it was like the moment people are encouraged to find in therapy where the adult self can go back and reassure the younger ... all Don could do was stare in horror at the reality of his memory.

Discussant The montage at the end is one of the most beautiful moments in Mad Men. It shows we are all exiles, living in Babylon – ie alienated in one way or another. And Rachel's definition of utopia as either "the good place, or the place that cannot be" suggests that there is no easy remedy to this alienation.

Dellamirandola Don's dismissive attitude to Betty's reminiscences about her mother is absolutely suffocating. He wants to live in the present (the big parallel in this episode is Roger and Joan), and for his own personal reasons doesn't like the idea of family nostalgia, but I agree with her on this one: it's perfectly normal for her to remember things her mother said to her, and Don is trying to make her feel that it's crazy. *And* he tells her to stop thinking about her family and think about him, the selfish bastard, which she dutifully does. Not that she needs much encouragement – this is the first episode where we see that Betty isn't just the domesticated little woman, she's also a sexual one who really, really lusts after Don.

Discussant Someone in the audience (at the coffee house) yells "take off your shirt" (towards a female performer). Even among the avant garde, sexism prevails, and we know that the sixties' social commitments will degenerate into a more self-regarding hedonism.

Nevada Canaries are caged for our enjoyment and this made me think of Maya Angelou's I Know Why the Caged Bird Sings with its look at racism, identity and displacement. So many of the MM characters are in cages of their own making or are kept in cages made for them. Watching what they do when they realize they can open the door and leave is one of the great pleasures of the show.

EPISODE SEVEN: Red In The Face

"At some point we've all parked in the wrong garage"
ROGER

When Roger dismisses JFK as "a boy, too scared to do anything but go on vacation," we get a glimpse of his own ennui. Both are rich, north-eastern boys with influential fathers, yet both were also second world war heroes who eventually cut their own paths. Very honourable. Rather less honourable is a lonely Roger inviting himself to the Drapers', getting incredibly drunk and eating Betty's steak (she settles for salad) before making a move on the hostess as the host hunts for more booze in the garage. Bad form, Roger, bad form.

The next day Roger tries to use the "unnatural sense of entitlement" that arises from having his name on the building as explanation for his bad behaviour. Don accepts his apologies, but crafts a fiendish scheme: revenge is a dish best served with a mignonette sauce. First, Don takes Roger out for a stomach-burning lunch, where he matches him for oysters and an ulcer-waking number of martinis. Then it's back to the office, where Don has bribed lift attendant Hollis into pretending the elevator is broken, meaning they have to climb the 23 floors to the Sterling Cooper offices. Red-in-the-face Roger looks close to death as he reaches the top – and upon meeting the Nixon team he projectile vomits his lunch on the plush carpets. It's punishment for Roger alright, but is it also a subtle sabotage of Bert's plans to help Nixon?

"Have you ever been hunting, Peggy?" PETE

Pete's slightly maniacal side seeps to the surface again when he is tasked with returning a horrific $22 (about $160 in 2010!) chip 'n' dip. After seeing an old alpha-male college buddy at the store – who refers to him as "Humps" as in Pete "The Camel" Campbell" – an emasculated Campbell fails to get the money back and instead uses the store credit to buy a rifle. He then waggles it around pointing it at various people in the office before the reliably deadpan Hildy removes it. It's further evidence of Pete's erratic tendencies.

Pete obviously harbours some kind of suffocated desire to return to the wild and hunt – his short story concerned a hunter and a bear and when he talks to Peggy in vivid terms about what he'd do with his prey the description is murderously sexual: "I'd cut it open, drain it, dress and then I'd take my big hunting knife and cut this loin right out of the side," he hisses. Peggy seems aroused, rather than alarmed by his threat to get his "big hunting knife out", purring "That would be wonderful". Trudy is rather less enthralled, we see her shouting at Pete off-screen for the purchase of the "stupid toy".

NOTES

- The incident with Glen comes back to haunt Betty with a contretemps in the supermarket with Helen, who evidently thinks she's some kind of child abuser.

- Roger infuriates Pete by wishing him: "Good night Paul."

- "You couldn't hit the side of (NYC's Catholic cathedral) St Patrick's with that," Pete is told when the boys see his gun.

- Peggy is running away with ideas for her copy but plays down her smarts to Pete: "Mr Rumsen liked what I did in the brainstorming 'thingy'."

20TH CENTURY TALES

- Lots of election talk in this episode as the "Nixon boys" pop in. Bert worries about having to move his piano if the famously ivory-tinkling Dicky himself was going to turn up.

- Two infamous Nixon incidents are brought up. Vice-president Nixon getting stoned by Venezuelans in Caracas in protest at US cold war policies in 1958 and his "practically shooting"

Helen Gahagan Douglas ("The Pink Lady") in the face to win the 1950 Californian senatorial elections.

- This episode originally aired in August 2007, as the Democratic primaries were warming up. The discussion of Nixon having been "sitting next to the leader of the free world" as opposed to young outsider Kennedy alluded nicely to the debates already raging over the varying suitabilities of Barack Obama and Hillary Clinton.

- Once more Pete is ahead of the game (and once more ignored) as he compares JFK's appeal to Elvis's.

- Roger got his commendation for bravery for fighting in the South China Sea in the battle of the Pacific.

CULTURE WATCH

- Pete was hanging out poolside with Norman Mailer and mayor Robert F Wagner. Or the "naked and the dead" as Kinsey called them in reference to the Mailer novel.

- At the restaurant, Don and Roger discuss I Love Lucy stars Lucille Ball and Desi Arnaz's divorce.

- The credits music is by Rosemary (aunt of George) Clooney: Botch-A-Me (Ba-Ba-Baciami Piccina).

- Roger quotes Jonathan Swift in the restaurant: "He was a bold man that first ate an oyster."

THOUGHTS FROM THE TYPING POOL

JoeDoone Betty is so desperate to emulate her mum in the looks department that she is flattered whenever a man looks at her, be it Dr Wayne looking down her neckline, Roger drunkenly pawing her up in the kitchen, or nine-year-old Glen telling her she looks like a princess and asking her for a lock of her hair. I'm with Helen Bishop on the last one; it's just weird for Betty to indulge such a weird request.

Bluewillow I loved the corny brassy end music of ... Baciami. This *was* the croony Clooney public sound and the beginnings of muzak too. It's the sound of offices and elevators and "waiting" in bars, and public places, which we don't really have anymore. It's not the tinny sound of pop or neutral tastefulness of "restaurant classical", but a humorous nightclub sound, grown-up and wholesome, and tacky all at once, but oddly uniting everyone like an aural comfort blanket.

Dellamirandola On rewatching, I stopped laughing and started getting morally outraged on Betty's behalf. To those who think she is childish: you realise you're agreeing with a dodgy psychiatrist who relies on now happily exploded theories about normality (which of course is male to him, the female is an inferior deviant)? For the second time Betty's character and what she has to experience come straight out of Betty Friedan and – in this episode specificially – her chapter on Freud. There's a whole thesis to be written on this series's use of Friedan both as a source and an explanation for the characters' behaviour.

We start with a psychiatrist talking about how she has the "emotions of a child", with "petty jealousies". We see how Betty infantilizes herself in her relationship with Don, and how he may get irritated by having a "child" to deal with but, in reality, is the person who really wants her in that childish box, so that she's not interfering with his autonomy. And it's Betty's acceptance of this role as the subordinate to the dominant men which means that she doesn't know what to do when Roger makes his move, because she's been playing the good wife to her husband's boss. What does Don think she should have done?

Immediately after this scene about "childish" Betty, we cut to Roger, the great baby, surrounded by the people who have been parenting him through his charmed life – whining at Mona "I *am* drinking my milk" and being told off by Bert for smoking too much.

EPISODE EIGHT: The Hobo Code

"I have all these things going on in my head and I can't say them." PETE

Has a show ever been so succinctly distilled as in this line from Pete? Campbell's revealing thought comes just before his second liaison with Peggy. Both come into the office early and, after an intimate chat, in which Pete reveals that his wife is just "another stranger" to him, we know what's about to transpire. Sort of. Pete is so sinister that when he whispers "close the door", he could either be about to seduce Peggy, or kill her. Later, Trudy arrives to drag Pete off to supervise the move to the couple's new flat; we see Campbell's manipulative powers in full swing as he manages to turn his guilty reaction to her appearance into her apologising for disturbing him at work.

Peggy is less riddled with this forlorn existentialism. The success of Don's pitch leaves her with a literal spring in her step. Her Belle Jolie "Mark Your Man" copy is strong, but a barnstorming bit of oratory about belief from Don – "I'm not telling you about Jesus. He either lives inside your heart or he doesn't" – seals the deal and leaves the office buzzing. Peggy is even invited into Don's office to celebrate. The team then head down to twist at PJ Clarke's, where Peggy steps out of Pete's creepy shadow and dances with her colleague. "I don't like you like this," he hisses at her – disgusted at himself for his lust. He wants someone to co-inhabit his puddle of suppressed ambition, but the more home runs this ballerina hits, the further away she'll pirouette.

"Ask me anything." DON

Like Andy Warhol, who owned every room he stood in but still felt like such an outsider that he hid behind a camera, Don is an outsider looking in. Not just into the unemotional free market world of his Rand-espousing boss (see below), but with Midge's beatnik chums. As the others get high, Don is using her

Instamatic to capture the moment. He's not adverse to the green stuff either and a few tokes see him flashing back to his youth.

There we meet a hobo (played by Paul Schulze) who is invited to stay the night and earn his keep. He teaches Don "the hobo code" and makes him "an honorary". The idea of ditching everything and travelling seems to have stuck with Don; as soon as Bert gives him his $2,500 bonus he goes straight to Midge's to persuade her to go to Paris with him. He's a wide-eyed wanderer, who ran from his family once, and could again.

Midge's friends don't know he's an itinerant child though, to them he's still all grey flannel. When one challenges him, two ideologies collide: "You make the lie, you invent want," Don is told. "There is no big lie, there is no system. The universe is indifferent," he replies. They're both right, but one is inclined to side with Don: he may have made the lie (principally of himself) but he seems resigned to living within an indifferent universe, rather than weakly challenging it and ultimately becoming part of the system, while the real revolution is being fought by the Peggys of the world. Ultimately, Don knows he's lost Midge to this world – when she won't go to Paris he gives her the cheque and runs home to hug his son.

"It's like you can do anything in New York." ELLIOTT

In case viewers hadn't twigged that Sal is the closeted gay character Weiner referred to when he was first promoting the show, the Hobo Code extrapolates. First, with Lois Sadler, a new girl in the switchboard, who – taken in by Sal's chats in Italian with his mother – makes a beeline to the art department to seek out her man, to no avail. Sal nips to the Roosevelt to "bump into" Belle Jolie's Elliott who's been speaking pleasingly about the hotel's renovation. They both know why they're there – and eventually Elliott invites Sal up to his room to see the view. But Sal's still in denial to himself, let alone other people and the rendezvous ends with Sal bottling it, and firmly reshutting the closet door.

NOTES

- When Don notices Peggy's ripped blouse she mentions that she "might start keeping a spare." Just like her boss.

- There's a very nice and literal visual metaphor with many characters people hiding things in drawers – Don is fond of the practice. Here Pete hides his glass of bourbon there when Trudy arrives.

20TH CENTURY TALES

- The red scare still lingers: "Don't put your name on a list … have you never heard of Joseph McCarthy?" asks one of the girls. "It's the bowling team," explains Lois.

- One of the men in Midge's flat attacks Don because ads won't "bring back those ten dead kids in Biloxi". A reference to Civil Rights deaths on the Mississippi Gulf Coast.

CULTURE WATCH

- Single Sal is compared by one of the switchboard gals to Ernest Borgnine's bachelor lead in 1955 Delbert Mann picture Marty.

- Bert proffers free market bible Ayn Rand's Atlas Shrugged to Don. He says flatteringly of Don that they embody Randian principles of being "completely self-interested" and "unsentimental about the people who depend on our hard work".

- One of the other books on Cooper's shelf was The Crisis of the Old Order by Arthur Schlesinger Jr. Schlesinger was in some ways an anti-Rand, and critic of free markets. This book documented the period of 1919-33, the first age of Roosevelt.

- At Midge's flat they're listening to Miles Davis's Concierto De Aranjuez (Adagio).

- Peggy dances with Freddie to the Rinky Dinks' awful Choo Choo Cha Cha but it's Chubby Checker's The Twist that really gets everyone – apart from Pete – dancing.

- The song playing over the credits is a bluegrass version of Old Time Religion.

THOUGHTS FROM THE TYPING POOL

JoeDoone One of the things which this episode emphasises is the rivalry between Peggy and Paul in the copywriting department, and the fact that Peggy, on her first outing, is praised, whereas Paul's work is mocked.

Superspartan Good point about Don actually having the kind of background that is often idealised by the beatniks (and folkies who followed) who reject him. There seemed to be an attitude that it was purer to be rootless, impoverished, etc and everyone wanted to be Woody Guthrie. Indeed, Bob Dylan even invented that kind of background for himself.

Nevada The whole thing may be an illustration of Rand's Atlas Shrugged. The flashback to Dick's childhood being a good example of rational selfishness. The hobo has abandoned a traditional life for one of no responsibility with no concern for the family left behind. Dick's father dishonestly refuses to pay the hobo for work done and is marked as dishonest in the hobo code. Don lives a life of rational selfishness and fundamental dishonesty yet promises to never lie to his son

Rand rejected faith and god. There are a number of references to religion and superstition throughout the episode. Trudy is superstitious about celebrating the move. Then there's Don's "you're a non-believer … I'm not here to tell you about Jesus" pitch. Which is described later as Don walking round the village three times and then setting fire to it – which sounds like casting a spell or Biblical vengence.

In the flashback, Dick is sent out to make sure the hobo says his prayers. To which he gets the chilling response, "praying won't help you in this place, kid … if death was any place, it's here".

DellaMirandola Last week we had lots of Betty Friedanesque ideas about women: this week we get Bert Cooper's Ayn Rand theory of masculinity. Men are productive, reasonable, unsentimental, hardworking, different from the lesser mortals they stride among. Do we think Don checks these boxes? I think he both wants to and is uncomfortable by Bert's saying this – partly because, as we see from his waiting outside Bert's office like a naughty schoolboy, he hasn't quite realised that he's at the top now.

Bluewillow I found the dynamic of Peggy dancing in the bar and Pete's disgust powerful and very real, in the organic way that reality is complex and irrational. His palpable, chemical aversion to her rang true from what I remember from immature boys in school, who ignored girls they had "conquered", and were subliminally cruel because they had developed no empathy yet alongside their power. I loved the subtlety of the writing there: there's no narrative need for him to be seen having that ugly reaction; and I understood it as him finding her looking so vulnerable on the dance floor (with no conventional armour of a date, or spouse), almost unbearable.

DellaMirandola [RE: The Crisis of the Old Order] That's a great spot! The Old Order is definitely in crisis in this episode, as Don, who still thinks he's a modern man, encounters the next generation. Pete's reaction to one new bit of the 1960s – the sexual energy as everyone dances to The Twist – relates to Don's reaction to its opposite, the beatniks getting high and listening to Miles.

EPISODE NINE: Shoot

"She wanted me to be beautiful so I could find a man. There's nothing wrong with that. But then what? Just sit and smoke and let it go until you're in a box?" BETTY

Don's pet name for his wife is Birdy – which highlights the metaphor at the heart of Shoot. For Betty, trapped in a suburban birdcage, the opportunity to break out and swoop back to a lost life as a Manhattan model is too good to turn down. But what Betty doesn't realise – sadly, given the extent to which she has been defined by her marriage – is that the offer to be a Grace Kelly-type for a new Coca-Cola advert is actually a ruse by Jim Hobart at McCann Erickson to try to hire her husband.

At the beginning of the episode we see the Drapers' neighbour Mr Beresford letting his pigeons out of their coop – by the end of the episode, when Don has worked out the scheme, one of the birds has been fatally wounded by a dog bite.

We see, via some wonderful acting from January Jones (also an ex-model) the hurt that this process causes Betty, who talks with pride about her former life, even showing off a dress made for her by an Italian designer in the days when she had to wrestle with her mother over her lifestyle. So when Betty gets the Coke ad we see her bloom in happiness (like Peggy when she got her copy job). This is who she *is*, not an Ossining housewife. Even Don seems happy for her – "Don't worry, I'm not going to ruin this for you" – until he realises that Betty has been a pawn. After a brief flutter, she ends up back in her coop, taking the kids to watch the swimming pool be filled; any suggestion that she's fine with the situation are erased in perhaps *the* iconic Mad Men scene where, with a Keef Richards-style fag hanging out of her mouth, Betty takes a rifle to Mr Beresford's birds. If she can't fly, why on earth should they?

"Who knew that college was going to get me out of the army and into laxatives?" HARRY

An old sorority tale leads Pete to a eureka moment on the Nixon campaign. If they flood the market in the marginal states with ads for Secor Laxatives then there will be no space for the Kennedy team to buy them. It's genius. When Bert storms into their meeting later, Harry and Pete reluctantly own up (or just about), assuming they're in for a shellacking for their, um, brown-sky thinking. But in fact it works – it's the kind of Machiavellian smarts that Pete excels at and, for once it turns out all right. Just when you're pleased for him, however, Pete rubs it in Don's face ("Peggy, can you write that down, Don said 'congratulations'") and tells poor Hildy "You should do something with that sourpuss". At least he makes up for his riveting obnoxiousness by suckerpunching Ken as he derides Peggy's derrière. Ouch.

"Belle Jolie was OK, but she obviously let it go to her head and other places." PAUL

A quick word on Peggy, who's put on a lot of weight; so much so that her clothes are beginning to rip. The boys speculate about whether she slimmed down before getting the job, while Joan tries to tell Peggy to curb her waistline. This leads to two wonderful moments: Pete's punch and a telling scene between Joan and Peggy, where Joan tells Peg she only got to work on an account because the men's wives wouldn't be jealous of her. Ouch. Peggy responds proudly that she's the first woman "to do any writing since the war" (when a generation of women broke the ground that Peggy is now wading through). Joan's belief that she was only doing it to get close to Paul is astonishing. Does she entirely believe it? Or is she just projecting her own insecurities and self-definition on to Peggy? Peg's bold response shows that the power has shifted to her, whatever the dress size.

NOTES

- We learn that Don met Betty on a photoshoot when "he was just a copywriter at the fur company".

- "I'm practically jealous of her," says Sal of Jackie Kennedy.

- An interesting insight into Roger's career conservatism when he's trying to keep Don: "Why entertain the prospect of failure?"

- Both Don and Betty carry matriarchal scars. First, Betty's nerves are struck when her shrink suggests she harbours anger towards her mother for calling her "stout" among other things. Then Don tells her "I would have given anything to have a mother like you." Which is why he's happy to keep her in this unreconstructed pre-Friedan role as a surrogate for the mother he never had.

20TH CENTURY TALES

- Betty mentions proto supermodel Suzy Parker, who was making $100,000 a year when Ms Draper was modelling.

- The boys watch a video of Jackie Kennedy appealing to Spanish-speaking voters *en español*. Harry Belafonte starred in a similar ad to woo black voters.

- Pete might have been right about the ad strategy, but not about the election result: "He [Nixon] can't lose with an eight point lead!"

CULTURE WATCH

- Don and Betty meet Jim Hobart from McCann at the Broadhurst theatre, where they're "enjoying" Fiorello!, the Pulitzer-winning musical about the work of the great reforming NYC mayor Fiorello LaGuardia.

- Betty goes on her shooting spree to Bobby Helms's My Special Angel.

THOUGHTS FROM THE TYPING POOL

Zanina Betty cannot take the rejection. When she talks to Don, she pretends that it was her choice not to do the campaign. He knows that she is lying, but he plays along, not willing to add to her distress. But denial does not work for Betty this time. She goes through the day, still in her nightgown, a sure sign of her depression. Until she finds the strength to express her anger toward an external object, the helpless birds … she is still metaphorically hitting at herself, and not directing her power outwardly. A beautiful ending to the episode.

Oldmuskrat Betty's relationship with her Italian admirer Giovanni ("Johnny") who made all those costumes for her has similarities to Grace Kelly, who was courted/had flings with fashion designer Oleg Cassini, later famed for Jackie K's pillbox hats. Also Grace Kelly had a very controlling mother who disapproved of her daughter's acting ambitions and modelling stint in Manhattan, exactly like Betty's.

BlueWillow I liked the artifice of the Coca-Cola ad colours, with its saccharine idealisation of family contrasted with the manipulation underpinning it, via Betty, the ad man's wife, drawn in by ruthless, bruising Madison Avenue machinations, remote from her own emotional innocence. Visually it reminded me of timidly sexualized Norman Rockwell illustrations, or desexualized Vargas figures. All deliberate references, to be sure.

DellaMirandola I think Joan is incapable of seeing the world otherwise than through the prism of sex/relationships/marriage – and that's her tragedy, because if she were able to ally her hard-nosed business sense to her use of her sexuality she would be a proto-Madonna (the pop singer, not the virgin). The idea that a woman's ambition in the workplace is about, you know, *work* and not snaring a man is just not something that she's ever thought about …

On Don and Betty's relationship – it's founded on *stuff*, with Don first wooing Betty with a fur coat, and attracted to her because of a glamorous image. And then at the end to validate staying in her box, she says "'look at all this", and to validate his keeping her in a box, he paints a glamorous picture of what she is. I found all their conversations where she is trying to ask his permission to go back to modelling and he doesn't want to give it, without either of them wanting to articulate that he has the power to give or withhold permission, absolutely agonising to watch for the way they conveyed all the subtextual unexpressed power dynamics.

EPISODE 10: Long Weekend

"All these years I thought it'd be the ulcer." ROGER

The contradiction that runs at the heart of Don Draper – philanderer, liar, fraud – is that he has a moral code. For Don, pleasure must be earned. So when he and Roger pick two fawning sisters up from the auditions for an aluminium advert and Roger coerces them into touching each other, Don's disquiet is visible. The sleaziness and abuse of position are one thing – but this is just *too* easy. After Don rebuffs the advances of Annabel, he's itching to leave. He never gets the chance though, as the years of booze, cigarettes and fatty food catch-up with Striling, and he has a heart attack during sex with Mirabelle. It's a jolt, but no surprise – John Slattery's pallid face as Don slaps his wife's name into his head on the stretcher is gruesome. And therein lies a lesson to Masters of the Universe such as Roger – they may control the world, but they must also control themselves: "I've been living the last 20 years like I'm on shore leave," reflects the sorry former sailor.

Don's reaction is to head to Rachel's flat. He looks distraught, perhaps having glimpsed his own future. "He's your friend isn't he?" asks Rachel. "What's the difference?" replies Don, the inference being that everyone dies, get used to it. But it is a protective shield he soon lets down – and Roger's brush with death gives him the motivation to plead that Rachel let him close to her: "This is it, this is all there is and I feel like it's slipping between my fingers like a handful of sand." Don also reveals he – like Rachel – is the child of a mother who died during birth and opens up about his father's death, and the fact that he was raised by "two sorry people". Don believes that these facts define him ("You know everything about me," he whispers). Has he found a soulmate in Rachel?

"We don't have a lot of men around here." JOAN

In a fascinating minor subplot we meet Carol, who tells her housemate, Joan, that she's utterly in love with her and has been since college. Joan – possibly to her credit – bats her off gently, telling her: "You've had a hard day." Incidentally Joan's line, "1960, I am so over you" seems a very fin de siècle phrase – and a very Carrie Bradshaw one. Which is fitting seeing as Joan and Carol's party lifestyle chimes with Mary McCarthy's The Group, Sex and the City's most famous precursor (and a key reference in series three). The Group also features one of the 60s' first major lesbian characters (Lakey) in a world where – culturally and socially – that weren't many role models for Carol.

It's a very sad scene. More so even than Sal's dinner with Elliott, because of the longevity of Carol's desire and the desperation of begging, "Joanie, just think of me as a boy." When Carol tells one of the sweaty men they bring back to their apartment to do "whatever you want" to her, she can't disguise her heartbreak.

NOTES

- Paul needs some help with his chat-up lines, using "Do you like Ukrainian food?" again on some of the aluminium girls.

- Don waits for Pete to leave, after they lose the Dr Scholl's

contract, in order to swipe clear his desk so he doesn't get the
furious reaction.

- More Randian cold-bloodedness from Cooper – rather than
visit Roger in hospital he calls in Joan to telegram clients to
say business won't be affected.

20TH CENTURY TALES

- The team watch a catchy Kennedy for Me ad. "Happy days
are here again," says Don in reference to Ager and Yellen's
Tin Pan Alley classic that FDR adopted as his campaign
theme in 1932. Harry describes it (unfortunately) thus: "It
gets inside your head and makes you want to blow your
brains out."

- "The president is a product, don't forget that," says Pete
wisely. Which doesn't help when they watch Nixon's
moribund ad about taxation.

- Kinsey's ditty ("Ethel, go get the ice-pick, that Nixon guy is on
TV again") may be a reference to the "ice pick" lobotomist
Walter Freeman (who gave JFK's little sister Rosemary a
lobotomy that left her incapacitated).

- Pete also suggests, with a Karl Rovian glee, smearing JFK. Don
and Roger (who else?) conclude that his reputation as a
womaniser will only help "push him over the top." They're
too slow anyway – by the time they get to the hospital JFK
has already launched his attack ads.

- Don sees a lot of himself in Nixon. And even says it. "Kennedy,
nouveau riche, recent immigrant who bought his way into
Harvard ... Nixon is from nothing, self made man who was
vice-president of the United States six years after getting out
of the navy. Kennedy, I see a silver spoon, Nixon, I see myself."
It's as close an admission to his poor roots as you'll get and
also a good dig at privileged Pete and Roger.

CULTURE WATCH

- Betty refers to Gloria waiting at the funeral like it was "some sort of Sadie Hawkins dance". This is a reference to the Lil' Abner comic strip in which the titular Sadie grew tired of waiting for a man to invite her to a dance and so reversed the trend. It lead to real dances over the US in which girls asked boys to dances rather than vice versa.

- Joan suggests Roger goes to see The Apartment to which he responds, "Oh please, a white elevator operator." Joan seems stung by Peggy's comments about her in the previous episode – she refers, erroneously to Shirley MacLaine's character being "handed around like a tray of canapes".

- Pete riffs on Peggy's sartorial inelegance by calling her "Howdy Dowdy" in a nod to cowboy puppet show Howdy Doody.

- Joan is stuck "somewhere between Doris Day in Pillow Talk and Midnight Lace." But what she needs to be "is Kim Novak in just about anything".

- Roger takes Mirabelle for "a ride" to the McGuire Sisters' version of Volare.

THOUGHTS FROM THE TYPING POOL

Joe Doone Roger references the recently-released La Dolce Vita by riding around on Mirabelle. If she had ridden around on him, he might not have survived the night.

UninspiredName Roger was doing a Jack Benny impression with the "Oh, Rochester!" line [towards Don], referring to Benny's valet on The Jack Benny Show. Which may also say something about how Roger sees Don.

Zanina I liked how Roger invites Don to this night of planned debauchery: "I can use you as bait". One of the elements of Roger and Don's friendship cum rivalry is a sexual competition (as apparent when Roger hits on Betty), but Don is younger, so he has the upper hand (and he knows it).

DellaMirandola I almost have more time for spoilt Roger than for the Don Draper school of morality: don't rock the boat, just radiate your disapproval. And cheating is cheating, it doesn't matter whether it's a casual fling or carried out with po-faced seriousness and a lot of angst about your terrible life.

Meanwhile Betty's father issues are paralleled with Rachel's: ultimately Rachel has some control and can both respect her father and do her own thing, while Betty yet again is in the childish box where all she can do is whine and not try to understand. And Carol finds that playing the good girl at work, properly subordinate to her boss, gets her fired, which is nicely juxtaposed with alpha male Roger's response to the loss of the Scholl account, "let's fire someone"

Nevada There's more on the theme that women are there for men's use and delectation: Gloria is here to serve and Carol is fired for covering up for her boss. Joan is resenting being used by men to boost their egos and The Apartment adds to it.

Joan gently dismisses Carol's protestations of love and says she wants to go eat, she's starving. Leaving poor Carol starving for Joanie. And they both go out on the town and come home with a boring unattractive middle-aged man. Why? Why is that better than staying home? It's so sad. Is this the ultimate fate for these girls if they don't marry – their equivalent of Roger's heart attack?

The Real Mad Men

Is the show a wry commentary on today's ad-land culture?

STEPHEN ARMSTRONG

When Peggy starts her secretarial job at Sterling Cooper, she is given some advice about her bosses. "They think they want a secretary. What they really want is a cross between their mother and a waitress."

She works for Don Draper, the creative director, played with impeccable style by Jon Hamm, who is always to be found cigarette in hand, eyes half closed and a suit so sharp you could cut yourself on its lapel. In attitudes and behaviour, Mad Men is a beautifully realised period piece. Draper tells a female client that love doesn't exist: it's a concept admen invented to sell pantyhose. A Jewish client is a big problem for the agency – they have to seek out the one Jew they employ to make her feel at home. They hit the booze tray in the late morning onwards. Gay people are in the closet; and girls are grateful there are men at IBM smart enough to design an electric typewriter simple enough for women to use. Peggy is told to show a bit of leg and give the men what they want – then she's sent off to a doctor so she can be prescribed the pill.

First aired in the US in July in 2007, it has already picked up two Golden Globes and several other awards. Weiner, who has also worked on The Sopranos, has insisted that this is not merely a condescending look back at a quaint and distant past. "You tell me if this is a period piece," he has said. "The men are asking: 'Is this it?' The women are asking: 'What's wrong with me?' You tell me if that sounds like it's 1960 or 2007."

But surely the advertising industry itself has moved on in the past 50 years? The five deadly sins – smoking, drinking, racism, adultery and sexism – can't play a part in the slick, modern communications industry that sprawls across metropolitan hotspots, can they? A quick vox pop of agency staff reveals the answer is not clearcut.

The sharp suits have been replaced by ironic T-shirts, the smoking has gone outside and the drinking has been relegated to after working hours. Yet there are still shockingly few ethnic minorities in the industry – 94% of adland employees in 2007 were white, according to the latest survey by the Institute of Practitioners in Advertising.

The picture for women is more complex. The Institute of Practitioners in Advertising's census for 2007 found that the gender split of people coming into advertising was roughly equal, explains Alison Hoad, vice-chair of Rainey Kelly Campbell Roalfe Y&R, Virgin Atlantic and Land Rover's agency, whose founding partners include MT Rainey, the first woman to have her name over the door of a British advertising agency. The same survey showed, however, that 80% of creative staff are men. "You'd hope this would have changed in the last 50 years – but it clearly hasn't," says Hoad.

"You still get the godlike male creative director surrounded by beautiful PAs and producers," agrees Philippa Roberts, co-founder of PrettyLittleHead, a consultancy that advises on advertising to women. "While women make 80% of all purchasing decisions, one-in-two women say they don't think manufacturers understand women in the real world. One-in-two women say that manufacturers try to sell them things by making them feel bad about themselves, and 68% say they can't identify with women used in advertising at all. While the female audience is a huge growth opportunity in markets like brown goods, technology and automotive, 71% of them believe that manufacturers only consider them interested in 'beauty and stuff for the home'."

Hoad's experience of visiting US agencies is radically different, finding many more female creative directors in the US. Perhaps this is, in part, due to a certain historical time-lag. While Mad Men deals with the glory years of Madison Avenue, when legendary agencies such as Doyle Dane Bernbach in effect invented modern advertising, Britain's adland mayhem peaked in the 1970s and 80s and many of its luminaries are still practising. In his book Get Smashed, Sam Delaney describes the exploits of luminaries such as Frank Lowe, Alan Parker, Sid Roberson, David Puttnam and John Webster. Creative teams would write pitches in the pub; high living and high expense accounts were rampant – as were most of the men.

Webster recalls a copywriter who propositioned every girl he met, writing "fancy a coffee later?" on a piece of card and holding it up against a window as women walked past in the street. One Frank Lowe story found in the book concerns a Christmas party at the agency Collett Dickenson Pearce (CDP) where the powerful account man found himself in a lift with a young PA. "Fancy a blowjob, Frank?" she is reputed to have asked. "What's in it for me?" he replied. CDP casting sessions involved the male teams calling in model after model and asking to see her vital assets – "We think you're right for this job, but we want to see your legs just to make sure." At Saatchi & Saatchi, Margaret Thatcher's PR guru, Tim Bell, used his chauffeur-driven car to go from the office to a restaurant 150 yards down the road.

"Some of the overt sexism is still there," agrees Margaret Johnson, CEO of Leagas Delaney, "but I have to say that women these days are probably just as bad as the men. It's not a PC culture by any means – anyone coming into an ad agency from a legal firm would be shocked by the banter – but a pretty, young, male graduate is likely to get exactly the same kind of attention from the women as a woman does from the men. There are some corridors in some agencies that young men are scared to walk down." One agency PA recalls a powerful female client chasing a young male creative around the agency party, dancing every dance with him and terrifying the living daylights out of him in the process. She later ensured he would be working on her account.

At the same time, the PA recalls her move into account management was accompanied by a senior account director lurching up to her at an office do and telling her that when she got her new job he wanted her on his team "so I can watch your arse walk in and out of my office every day". He then slipped his thumb into the back pocket of her jeans. "He was one of the old guard," she shrugs.

Drinking culture, at first ask, appears to have diminished as agency margins got tighter and expense account belts tightened. And then the stories start to come out, some of which would slot quite neatly into an Adland Uncovered documentary on Sky.

"A mate of mine was out with his team very drunk, went to the toilet, came back and found they'd all cleared off after writing 'John, you're a nightmare!' on the table," says one junior creative. "People work very hard on pitches and then they like to let off steam. Most people in advertising are young, there's lots of client entertaining – it's not an industry for wallflowers." The creative hotshop Mother has an annual skiing trip where all the staff from every office around the world meet up for a week of ski – or rather, après-ski. J Walter Thompson and Grey both have bars inside their agencies.

Adultery seems to have slipped way down the list, although one media director confided that, after two divorces over infidelity at the office, alimony payments meant his take-home pay was less than his salary as a trainee.

There is one clear difference, however. No one smokes any more. Or at least, they have to do it on the pavement these days.

What the real life Mad Men think of the show

Sir John Hegarty, worldwide creative director of BBH
"It's a fantastic series and I can certainly remember when every director had a drinks cabinet in his office and smoking was everywhere. What's clever is that they've woven real advertising from the era into the plots. In the first series they discuss Doyle

Dane Bernbach's famous Volkswagen Beetle ad called Lemon. Bernbach laid the foundations of modern creative advertising. The industry was all about 'irresponsible optimism' before he emerged as a prophet, saying if you don't base your advertising on some truth then it will fail – just make the truth interesting."

Robin Wight, president of Engine and WCRS
"Mad Men captures the last hooray of the dinosaurs about to be challenged by the new generation who were to invent modern advertising in the 1960s. In fact, the Mad Men were even madder than on the show. Alcohol flowed freely: I was offered a huge martini at 3pm in my first job interview in 1965. The boardroom table of my first agency was used as a ping-pong table, and the receptionist, I discovered years later, doubled as a hooker. But it wasn't this alone that brought this world to an end; the adverts it produced weren't very good. The new agencies used wit and imagination rather than bullying hard sell."

Mark Lund, chief executive of DLKW and chairman of the Advertising Association
"Mad Men is a hymn to the power of confidence, which is still key to creating a good advertising campaign today. The characters have an innate belief that they can remake a company's fortunes or a brand's image and are prepared to make that bold jump into the unknown. Like all good social drama it compresses the incidents of 10 years into a week. But did they drink, smoke and fornicate a lot back then? Yes! Is there less of that now? Almost certainly. You can say that's a good or a bad thing, but it looks like fun doesn't it?"

Nicola Mendelsohn, chair and partner of Karmarama and president of Women in Advertising and Communications London
"I'm a huge fan. The styling is drop-dead gorgeous. It whisks you straight back to the early 1960s. Yes, there was racism and

sexism in the business, but that was because it existed throughout society, and advertising reflects the world around it. If you walked into an agency today you would find a very different scenario. There'd be more women, many in the top jobs. We'd still be doing essentially the same work, solving marketing problems, but we wouldn't be swigging whisky and smoking fags while we're at it."

Lord Tim Bell, chair of Chime Communications
"It is a glamorous, hyperbolised version of what agencies were like at the time. It's exaggerated because that's what TV does and that's what we want it to do. Reality can be dull. Has advertising changed? Yes, it has become much more serious and less fun. People do not have the same sense of drama. But isn't that always the way? Any new industry is more exciting when it first starts up – then it becomes just like any other."

Interviews by Imogen Carter and Lisa O'Kelly

EPISODE 11: Indian Summer

"The Rejuvenator. You'll love the way it makes you feel."
PEGGY

Repression is a tool that Mad Men's writers have sewn into almost every character's seams. Its two lead women are particularly afflicted. One emotionally and sexually as her husband cavorts in the city; the other by forces of class and office chauvinism. Indian Summer sees the two find interesting ways to deal with their frustration.

First, Peggy. After her successful bit of copywriting, she's itching to do more. When Pete is lumbered with an "electriciser" (passive exercise machine pants) account, the boys hand it over to the increasingly stout Olson to brainstorm some ideas. "You'd be perfect for it," says Freddy.

Peggy's discovery that the vibrating pants are more stimulating than exercising leads to her first real test as a copywriter. First she has to tell Don that their USP isn't their slimming effect, but a masturbatory one. Then she has to present it to the smirking boys and convince them that they can flog it slyly as a vibrator. Interspersed with this is an insight into her world back in Brooklyn, where her mother has set her up with truck driver Carl Winter. Peg, now seeing herself as a NYC sophisticate ("There's a bar in Manhattan where the glasses are chilled"), is dismissive of him, aligning herself with her Waspy betters. When Carl calls her out on it, she reveals her desire to step up a social notch: "Those people in Manhattan are better than us, because they want things they haven't seen."

Peggy is tantalisingly close to the elites – she sees "my friend Joan" cavorting around Manhattan and cocktail-sipping Don living the high life and desperately wants in. Who could blame her? She's not there yet – though a few more presentations like the one she gave to sell "The Rejuvenator" and she might be. Don is obviously admiring – he sees himself in her – and the first thing he does on reaching partnership is give her a pay rise. She celebrates with a bit of night-time textbook reading. In the "exercise" pants.

Meanwhile, Betty, another of Mad Men's repressed women, is reduced to getting her kicks during the scorching autumn weather from an air-con salesman. She invites him into the house and nearly escorts him up to the bedroom before thinking better of it. With a wicked flash in her eyes, she later tells Don about the incident, to induce some jealousy. It works, but not enough to ignite any intimacy. The next time we see her, she, like Peggy, is making use of a domestic item for altogether fruitier purpose. Intimacy with her husband is replaced by – cruel irony – a machine for doing housework.

"Beware the non-conformist." BERT

Things are becoming pretty tip-top for Don – his affair with Rachel is tickety-boo and Roger's absence leads Bert to promote him to partner (with a 12% stake). But unbeknown to him, across town his half-brother has hanged himself. There's more on this to come (especially with Pete nabbing the box Adam sent to Don), but for now let's look at Bert.

We saw some cold-hearted capitalism when Roger had his heart attack and he focused on how it would affect their business. It comes back to the fore here. He drags Roger into the office to reassure the Garners from Lucky Strike even though "he looks like death", leaving Roger to put on a facade of good health in order to keep the contract. Inevitably Roger keels over again as he's about to light up a fag. "I used to think you could never put a value on a human life, but I never asked Bert Cooper, did I?" sighs Mona. Bert's reaction? To tell Lee Garner that Don has everything under control. We also learn that his Ayn Rand fetish has increased to the point that not only does he share her philosophies of rational self-interest but he's become social pals with the writer: "I'm going to introduce you to Mrs Ayn Rand. I think she'll salivate," he tells Don.

NOTES

- Peggy lives in Prospect Park – then a deteriorating Brooklyn suburb, about to be invaded by hippies seeking cheap rents, now one of the most desired areas in New York.

- "You are the finest pice of ass I ever had," says Roger to Joan on his return. No regrets about his affairs then.

20TH CENTURY TALES

- "We should have done this for Nixon, before the debates." Roger is referring to the oft-cited sweaty appearance of Nixon in the debates that allegedly lost him a debate on television that he won on the radio.

CULTURE WATCH

- "Are you going to draw freckles on me too like [the doll] Raggedy Andy?" asks Roger while being made up by Joan.

- Betty is reading Family Circle magazine in bed while she waits for Don to return.

- Don and Betty are watching hit sitcom The Danny Thomas Show.

- Betty "does the washing" to Astrud Gilberto's take on bossa nova classic Agua de Beber.

- Peggy "flies to the moon" to the tones of Julie London.

THOUGHTS FROM THE TYPING POOL

Zanina There's some nice development of the relationship between Don and Peggy in this episode. He gives her the new assignment; mentors her about writing after she has made her pitch to him; helps her out when she is asked in front of the guys to explain what the machine really does; checks on her afterwards ("see, it wasn't that bad"); tells her to be more assertive when she asks for a raise; finally tells her in a fatherly way to take a break from work and go celebrate her success. It is probably the healthiest relationship Don has with anyone.

Oldmuskrat I like Peggy's choice of a Brandy Alexander (cognac with cream) during her dinner date with the Carl. Not often seen on the cocktail menu nowadays. It was the favourite drink of Alexander Woollcott, drama critic of the New Yorker and member of the Algonquin set (he was fond of claiming the drink was named after him). I think she probably had one once (ordered for her by Joan) but she's out to impress her date here with her sophisticated Manhattan ways. His choice of a cold beer is much more sensible

JoeDoone Don's line that, "It gives the pleasures of a man. Without the man" eventually hits the spot with independently-minded Peggy who wants to be footloose and fancy free in Manhattan and definitely not tied down to a truck driver. Peggy's remark that the USP of the orgasmopants is "probably unrelated to weight loss" is a masterpiece of understatement and evasion.

Nevada After her success, Peggy has been to the library and I think she's reading the classic Scientific Advertising by Claude C Hopkins which looks at testing and measuring the success of adverts. This will help her counter the sort of challenges to her profession that her date made. She's serious about her work.

Oldmuskrat I suppose Lucky Strike is SC's main meal ticket and he feels he has to haul Roger back in the boardroom in order to assuage Lee Garner's fears. Garner is obviously a pain, he makes a joke about checking the cigarette stubs in the ash tray, "They're all ours!", but it shows his underlying paranoia (Ed: See Jerry Della Femina talking about the real Lee Garner, George Washington Hill on page 76).

DellaMirandola Oh the delicious irony of Pete sitting at Don's desk pretending to be Don, and thus handed the evidence that Don is only pretending to be Don...

The theme about the lure of the big city which runs through the first series gets an airing in the form of Peggy's date. They both get a sympathetic portrayal. Yes, Peggy is overflowing about her glamorous life in the city which we know is fake ("my friend Joan" indeed), but are your sympathies really with the truck driver who's happy with his lot or with the girl who yearns to be one of "those people in Manhattan"? There are so many dramas that knock out a theme of "home is best, know your place" that Mad Men's insistence on showing how home is limiting and impoverished in one way or another is very refreshing.

EPISODE 12: Kennedy v Nixon

"The Japanese have a saying. A man is whatever room he is in." BERT

Against a backdrop of Kennedy v Nixon and the post-election power grab, a similar struggle is being played out at Sterling Cooper – although the result is very different. Don Draper, who in Long Weekend compared himself to self-made man Nixon, rather than Kennedy, a Massachusetts trustafarian, finds himself in opposition with the privileged inhabitants of his office – and particularly young upstart Pete Campbell.

While the rest of the office swig crème de menthe from the water coolers and make whoopee on the sofas, Pete is at home, rifling through the box of old pictures of Don/Dick that he intercepted. As he realises that Don can't be who he says he is, Campbell turns to some basic game theory. Campbell wants to be head of accounts. Don is making that decision. He has some prize dirt on Don. Is it worth the risk to threaten him?

Don certainly seems worried by Pete's attempt at blackmail, heading to Rachel Menken's and – in true hobo spirit – trying to persuade her to run away with him. But some plants have strong roots: once Rachel realises that Don is prepared to ditch his kids and bail she tells him to leave. It's only when Don returns to his office and hears Peggy crying "People who are not good get to walk around doing anything they want" that he decides he's not going to let Campbell do what *he* wants.

Pete's plea after Don tells him he's going to hire Duck Phillips (from Young & Rubicam) is a familiar one: "Why can't you give me what I want?" Throughout the show he makes this complaint of Don, his wife and his family, anyone. Why should they? Don certainly won't – preferring to blow himself up rather than kowtow to Pete.

The more cunning might remember here that 1) Don is a hardy opponent who's dragged himself from the fur factory to the top of the ad world and 2) No one likes a grass. The super-cunning would realise that a neo-liberal free marketeer like Bert Cooper wouldn't care who this man is, just so long as said man can make him money. Pete might be weasely, but his cunning isn't quite ratlike yet. And so after a Mexican stand-off in Cooper's office, Bert laughs off Pete's story, Don gets away with it (though his secret is out) and Pete is left to stew. "Don, fire him if you want. But I'd keep an eye on him. One never knows how loyalty is born," muses Bert. Don returns home, just in time to see his alter-ego Nixon concede defeat.

"You got your whole life ahead of you, forget that boy in the box." WOMAN ON TRAIN

Interspersed with this are a couple of very important flashbacks that reveal how Dick became Don. We learn that, while building a hospital in Korea, an explosion caused by Dick killed the real Don (Draper's commanding officer), disfiguring him so badly that Dick had a chance to swap dog tags with the soon-to-be-discharged Draper. As no one knew what Dick Whitman looked like, he was free to return to America and be reborn. As he escorts "his" body back home, he's bought a drink by a woman who likes a man in uniform. And thus, a rascal is born. This is perhaps the most important narrative point of series one – the mystery that's supposed to have hooked us in – but it's testament to the show's qualities as an exploration of the period that after the first watch it seems almost as unimportant to the viewer as it does to Cooper. There's so much more going on here than the mysterious background of Donald Draper.

NOTES

- Don tells his daughter Sally: "I don't think that's a conversation that's appropriate for children" when she asks what the electoral college is. Is it possible that he doesn't really know either?

- I loved the jump between Ken meanly outing Paul's ambitions as a playwright to the staff eagerly acting out scenes from "Death Is A Client: A Play in One Act by Paul Kinsey".

- Someone needs to give Kinsey a lesson in the art of the roman-à-clef mind. "I can't control my genius. I'm not some boyish natural like that hack Cosgrove," reads one line.

- Seems like SC lost the Nixon work. Bert, as ever is pragmatic: "Neil from P&G said that if Kennedy is willing to buy an election, he's probably willing to play ball with us."

- Jane and Paul "Chekhov" Kinsey had a romantic past, but the smooth operator ruined things by blabbing about his conquest to the rest of the office.

- Following in their footsteps are the married Harry and Hildy (Pete's secretary) who share an election night of passion and a horribly awkward morning after.

20TH CENTURY TALES

- "I've read three different newspapers with three different results," bemoans Don. 1960 was, like 2000, famously close. A shift of 4,500 voters in Illinois and 28,000 in Texas would have turned both states red and given Nixon victory. Hence Nixon not conceding until Don returns home the evening after the election.

- Also like 2000, allegations of voter fraud were rife. Bert refers to suggestions that the Kennedy campaign stole votes in notoriously corrupt Illinois.

- Nevertheless, Bert, unaided by hindsight, thinks that Tricky Dicky's fight will see him run again. Apparently he did ...

CULTURE WATCH

- Harry was planning to spend the election night watching the Walter Lang-directed film version of Cole Porter's musical Can

Can with his wife. The film starred Shirley MacLaine and Frank Sinatra. Speaking of whom …

- "When they got Frank Sinatra, I knew they would close the gap," says Bert Cooper of Ol' Blue Eyes's contribution to the JFK campaign, a reworking of his hit High Hopes.

- When Peggy is castigating Sal, Ken and Paul, Paul notes a "striking resemblance to Broderick Crawford", star of TV police drama Highway Patrol.

- Yma Sumac's Gopher Mambo plays as Ken is chasing Alison around the office and showing the office the colour of her knickers. "I used to think I'd find a husband here," muses one of the secretaries.

THOUGHTS FROM THE TYPING POOL

Zanina A quote from Helen Gurley Brown illuminates the shenanigans in the office on election night. They come from an op-ed in the Wall Street Journal in 1991, when Supreme Court nominee Clarence Hill had been accused of sexual harassment: "When I was working my way through secretarial school in Los Angeles at radio station KHJ, and I came in from school every afternoon, some of the men would be playing a dandy game called Scuttle. Rules: All announcers and engineers who weren't busy would select a secretary, chase her down the halls, through the music library and back to the announcing booths, catch her and take her panties off."

Oldmuskrat Bert's Japanese saying "a man *is* whatever room he is in…" is nice and Zen sounding with a twist of existentialism, but I think something's got lost in translation. I have consulted my Japanese expert who has in turn consulted Yahoo Japan and a few Japanese *MM* fans are scratching their heads as a result. The closest one is about a man needing half a tatami mat when standing and a whole tatami mat when lying down, ie, adapting to circumstances in life and a rejection of furnishings/

possessions/emotional baggage. Another one is "If you look at the house, you understand the man". There are less vague ones that hit the button too such as "A liar is the beginning of a thief" (watch out Don); "The fish you fail to catch is always big," (which could apply to Pete) and my favourite, "Even a pig will climb a tree if you flatter him enough." I think Bert uses that one all the time.

Nevada Don Mark II is the embodiment of the American Dream, a self-created man born from the grisly ashes of Don Mark I. The first Don dreamed of returning home to build swimming pools. His reincarnation has made a huge leap from rural poverty to rich NYC businessman in ten years. People go to America to be what they can't be in the old country – perhaps a man is whatever country he is in. Dick left America to escape who and what he was there and returns a new man.

DellaMirandola It is actually very bizarre to see so many people *wanting* Nixon to win. How are we supposed to feel about it? Are we supposed to be thinking "… ah if only they knew", or are we supposed to see that Don has a point about Nixon being the guy who sweated his way to the top through the school of hard knocks? It's interesting that Don's opinion is that Nixon is *real*, yet of course we know now that he always was a slimy bastard, and Don himself is here choosing as an avatar/hero someone who isn't really like himself. He *didn't*, as Nixon did, remain imprisoned by the traumatic stern family upbringing, and he didn't get where he is today through hard work but through a lucky break. Is Don really Kennedy, the master of PR, and being "Kennedy" by virtue not of hard work and deeds but by being the perfect construct to fill the role of "Kennedy" the dashing young politician with the wife and family – and of course the man who got a significant break in his career through a fortuitous (yet traumatic) wartime accident that made people think he was a hero? Nixon v Kennedy is that past-ridden loser Dick Whitman versus that shiny success Don Draper.

The Last Mad Man Standing

Jerry Della Femina's cult account of the 60s ad world became one of the key influences on Mad Men. He describes the world of the real-life Sterling Coopers

WILL DEAN

He could be any of them. He's the working-class Brooklynite who rose from a lowly admin role to becoming one of the most respected names in advertising; he's Peggy Olson. He's the door-to-door salesman who went from obscurity to being one of the biggest names in New York adland; he's Don Draper. He's the old man running the firm, arguing with people about Ayn Rand; he's Bert Cooper. Yes, he's all of them and yet none of them. But Madison Avenue legend Jerry Della Femina might well be the last Mad Man standing.

In 1970, Della Femina, then the 34-year-old chairman of his own ad agency, wrote one of the defining books about advertising, the cult bestseller From The Wonderful Folks That Brought You Pearl Harbor. Its frank tone and daft anecdotes about the madness of 60s advertising made it a key source for Mad Men creator Matthew Weiner when building the world of Sterling Cooper.

Now that he's a doyen of the industry, Della Femina's book is being reissued to sate our hunger for stories from the 1960s ad world awoken by Mad Men. Della Femina worked with the team from the show on its launch, telling TV critics at a New York restaurant: "We made Mad Men look like [Shirley Temple musical] Rebecca Of Sunnybrook Farm. We were much wilder, we drank more, we carried on more."

Having struggled for years to break into the business – and having been told by venerable agency J Walter Thompson, established 1877, that it didn't want "your kind" [ie an Italian] – he finally made it in in 1961. Eight years later, when New York Times journalist Charles Sopkin trawled Madison Avenue looking for the new creatives, only one didn't care about being quoted. When the article, headlined What A Tough Young Kid With Fegataccio Can Do On Madison Avenue, was published, Della Femina found his name known beyond the gossipy world of advertising. It led to Sopkin ghosting Della Femina's adland tales for the book which became From Those Wonderful Folks Who Brought You Pearl Harbour. Its title comes from a suggestion Jerry made to colleagues for a line to sell Panasonic TVs.

The sea-change that Della Femina was part of is portrayed in series two of Mad Men when Sterling Cooper hires two brash young creative types, Kurt and Smitty, who immediately make the Ivy League old guard nervous. Doors for the likes of him were opened by the success of the brilliant (and Jewish) firm Doyle Dane Bernbach, whose elegantly counterintuitive VW Lemon ads ("We pick the lemons, you get the plums"), baffled Don and co in series one.

"If you look at Mad Men, it's set in the wrong decade," Della Femina explains. "The style of Mad Men is really the 1950s, not the 1960s. By the 60s there was a creative revolution and it was the most wonderful time, and that's what I talk about in my book, the wildness and the insanity of the 1960s. It was really based on people who thought that they'd never have a proper job suddenly finding themselves earning 40, 50, 60, 70,000 dollars."

Even in the original New York Times piece Della Femina had established himself as a maverick: "He perceived … that any deviation from the norm of behaviour would be bound to attract attention," wrote Sopkin. Among the choice tales in the book are Della Femina attacking the head of his firm over an unused ad; taking a whole creative department out on strike until he got an ad running in The New York Times magazine; and spending his original agency's last few thousand dollars on a blowout designed to make them look successful. It earned him three new accounts.

Most of the original Mad Men are long gone, but now in his mid-70s, Della Femina is still holding forth. "Let's face it: in advertising, you are paid more but you die younger," he says. "It was a business in which people burned out very young. It's not very forgiving. Like sports stars, you're in it during your better years and then you're out looking for work."

And Della Femina was often looking for work. Having dashed between agencies in the 60s, he decided to set up his own company "because I was going to be one of those people who would become hardcore unemployable". Forty years later, does he now see himself as a sage head like Mad Men's Bert Cooper? "Oh no, I always will be Don Draper. I gotta be involved; I still write ads, I still run around and rally the creative people. When it's too quiet, I'm the one who turns the music up loud. I just can't wait until they make [the book] into a movie ... I see Meryl Streep in my role!"

EPISODE 13: The Wheel

"Round and round and back home again to a place where we know we are loved." DON

The final episode of the first, magnificent, season of Mad Men chooses not to wrap things up but further tear at the decorative paper. With a fantastic bit of salesmanship from Don, a moment of honesty from Betty and a "what the?" plot lurch for Peggy, it's a captivating ending.

First Don. We've seen his ability to hide behind a camera lens in busy rooms – an observer in a world in which he's merely an image. Here, it's what's reflected back into the lens that's important, as Don is tasked with selling a Kodak projector in a competitive pitch. His solution? To load the device up with pictures of his beautiful family and make it a wheel of good fortune, before delivering a pitch worth a thousand Kodak moments:

> *"Nostalgia means 'the pain from an old wound'. It's a twinge in your heart far more powerful than memory alone. This device isn't a spaceship, it's a time machine. It goes backwards. Forwards. It takes us to a place where we ache to go again."*

The images of the young Draper family and Don's tender words are inspired by his own lack of participation in his family's lives. He's missing Thanksgiving to work and has just learned that his half-brother hanged himself in the squalor of a Times Square hotel. It's a gut-wrenchingly emotive scene. Indeed Harry, who's been washing in a bin in his office, having been booted out of his home, is moved to tears. The misery doesn't let up: having reminded himself what he's lucky enough to have, Don returns home not to his imagined happy family, but the reality of an empty house and a mistress who has disappeared halfway around the world to escape him. Suffice to say the pitch works – Kodak don't even bother to meet the wunderkinder at Doyle Dane Bernbach – and Don manages to bring the creaking Sterling Cooper back into the 1960s.

We've learned the specific facts of Don's existence over these first 13 episodes – but it's this moment that really gives him a heart and soul and gives us the motivation to root for a cheating, lying, deserter.

"How could someone do that to the person they love ... doesn't this all mean anything?" BETTY

What Don doesn't know during all of that is that just as he comes to realise how important home is, his wife, inspired by Francine's rumbling of Carlton's affairs, is on to him. Using the phone bill to discover that Don has been liaising with her shrink, Dr Wayne, she finally talks to her husband through the proxy of the doctor. She's not the naif we might have thought – she knows Don is a shagger – and she's finally willing to admit it. To herself as much as anyone:

"He's kind inside, but outside it's all there on his face every day. The hotel rooms. Sometimes perfume. Or worse."

This might be as close as Betty can get to confronting Don, assuming that lines like "I can't help but think I would be happy if my husband was faithful to me," will leak back to Wayne's co-conspirator. The walls built around her are now as visible as ever. The question is, will she try to knock them down or carry on putting up with it like, as she says, "some ostrich"?

"She was like Kinsey with balls." KEN

Peggy – our representative of the Betty Friedan wave of feminism – furthers that idea tonight. A strong performance directing the voice actors for the Relaxerciser combined with Pete's snaring of the Clearasil account give Don reason to promote her to the role of junior copywriter. (How much of that is based on a desire to spite Pete we don't know, but Don definitely rates her.) Most other shows would allow her journey from nervy secretary to stern ad woman to be a fulfilling enough narrative. But it soon becomes clear that the change in Peggy's appearance and shots of her craving food were to do with something else – something that keeps the glass ceiling very firmly in place ... she was pregnant. With what we can only presume is Pete's child. Having worked so hard to escape Brooklyn, the adminstrative work she can't stand and the snipes of the men above her, she's thrown right back off the cliff. When the baby arrives – she can't even look at it.

NOTES

- Pete seems to have exchanged a tacit promise to bring the Vogels a grandchild in exchange for the Clearasil account. You wonder if he even needs Bert's gift to him of an Ayn Rand novel.

- How did Harry's wife Jennifer find out about his sleeping with Hildy? His conscience must have got the better of him.

- Just as Bert's all-seeing eye knew about Joan and Bert, he's immediately on to Don and Rachel. "That's it cowboy," he warns his partner.

20TH CENTURY TALES

- Pete's father-in-law Tom assures him that because the Washington Redskins lost their last home game before the election, the incumbents (Nixon's Republicans) had to lose the election. Remarkably this stat remained true until 2004 when the Redskins lost to Pittsburgh, thus predicting a John Kerry win.

- Tom's company, Vick Chemical, has just bought Clearasil. "There's a surge in adolescence" he tells Pete in reference to the coming-of-age of the baby boomers. Clearasil – among thousands of other products – was cleverly marketed by the likes of Pete specifically to be sold to spotty teenage oiks during commercials for shows like Dick Clark's American Bandstand.

CULTURE WATCH

- During Harry's sad little heart-to-heart with Don he reveals his photographic side from his days at university in Wisconsin. "I did a whole series that was just handprints on glass." He also mentions that he was "always fascinated by the cave paintings of Lascaux. I thought it was like someone reaching through the stone."

- A clue to the year in which season two is set comes in the beautiful closing shot, as 1962's breakout star Bob Dylan's Don't Think Twice, It's Alright plays as Don sits and wonders why on the stairs. Is the key line: "I once loved a woman, a child I'm told. I gave her my heart but she wanted my soul"?

THOUGHTS FROM THE TYPING POOL

JoeDoone This episode is full of notions of fidelity and family and marriage. Pete has been unfaithful to Trudy. Carlton has been unfaithful to Francine, who consults Betty on the grounds that Betty must know what it is like to be married to a hound; Betty does know, but she has been suppressing the knowledge. Harry's cheating has been very much out of character and he is desperate to get back with Jennifer; he will even give up smoking. But his exile means that he is there to give Don the basis of a great idea, with the notion of hand paintings reaching through time.

ElectricDragon The episode is titled The Wheel, referring to the projector wheel, but also echoing Boethius' Wheel of Fortune – "as the wheel turns those that have power and wealth will turn to dust; men may rise from poverty and hunger to greatness, while those who are great may fall with the turn of the wheel." Or as Christopher Eccleston [as a homeless Boethius] declaims in 24 Hour Party People: "It's my belief that history is a wheel. 'Inconsistency is my very essence,' says the wheel. 'Rise up on my spokes if you like, but don't complain when you are cast back down into the depths. Good times pass away, but then so do the bad. Mutability is our tragedy, but it is also our hope. The worst of times, like the best, are always passing away'." Don is always trying to make the times pass away, and advising the same of others (such as Peggy).

ArundelXVI "It's not a wheel, it's a carousel." What an amazing, iconic scene. It distills the essence not only of Don Draper – his uncanny powers of persuasion – but of the show itself in a way. For many people of my sort of age (35+) with parents who were young in the 1960s, it evokes a powerful atavistic feeling, a nostalgia of those old color slides, a moving glimpse, in its incredible detail, of the lives our parents led when they were young. The world they lived in. This scene still moves me.

Oldmuskrat It's interesting this use of Latin and by both Don and Peggy [Don riffs on the meaning of nostalgia, Peggy on the root of the word rejuvenate]. Neither of them has had a classical education. In Britain, a classical education has always had a snobby cachet and the occasional judicious use of the Greek/Latin tag etc always came in handy for put downs aimed at uppity but lesser educated work colleagues.

Nevada The baby story is believable and pertinent. It's Peggy's equivalent of Dick's transformation into Don. Both are faced with an unexpected decision; an act of betrayal to enable them to reach their similar goals. Both will carry the knowledge of what they have done for ever and both will for ever fear its exposure. Peggy denies her baby and Don denies his half-brother because both tether them to lives they long to escape. Peggy and Don seek the American Dream and are prepared to abandon their closest relative to reach it. Time's wheel will tell if it's worth it.

Inside the Hard Sell: how Mad Men rewrote some classic pitches

JERRY DELLA FEMINA

LUCKY STRIKE: 'IT'S TOASTED!'

It's episode one and Don Draper is struggling to sell a new campaign to Lucky Strike. Just as the client gets up to leave, Sterling Cooper's finest pulls a line out of the bag.

"This is based on one of the great killers of advertising, a man named George Washington Hill, who ran Lucky Strike cigarettes. He destroyed advertising agencies; he was a terrible man. I've seen people do this, where they just catch on to something. Look at the drama. He doesn't just talk about cigarette smoke, there's an emotional point. You gotta reach out and be an actor. He [Jon Hamm] is an actor playing an actor. These people are like evangelists when they talk, when he says 'It's Toasted!'

"I once had to make up some body copy on the spot or risk losing a job for Bolex cameras. I picked up a blank piece of paper and preceded to read that it was 'about your children and how they grow up and you miss those moments …' I must say it was beautiful copy. I looked across and the guy was starting to tear up. I put it down and he says, 'I love it, we're sold!' We get out and my partner says, 'Do you remember what you just said?' I couldn't remember a word. We never came close to my copy. That's what happens in these meetings, they're wonderful."

KODAK: 'IT'S NOT A WHEEL, IT'S A CAROUSEL'

Pictures of Don's family inspire him to conjure a pitch that's so good a colleague leaves the meeting in tears.

"This pitch is magic, when he says, 'It's not a wheel, it's a carousel', look at the way he does it. He's thinking as he's talking, just measuring his words and going for the greatest dramatic effect. And this is how you do it, because when they leave your company at a new-business meeting, they're going to go to another company. It's one performance against another performance. Don's good, he's really good. I've seen people like him. People who can present and literally bring tears to people's eyes. It's an art. Don thinks on his feet and he grasps on to something.

"There's nothing like playing a client's thoughts right back to them in a different way with different words. There's something that goes on in a new-business meeting that's wonderful to watch. It's like showtime. There are people who are nervous and there are people who are jittery and there's so much drama and so much at stake. You can't believe how nervous people can be. And then the lights go down and you've got an hour or two to make the presentation and you better be good because the competition is like the theatre; there's a lot of other shows."

BELLE JOLIE 'MARK YOUR MAN'

Don is pitching Peggy Olson's first copy to a lipstick company who won't take his advice. So he stops the presentation.

"I have turned away clients almost under the same [circumstances]. When we were first starting out and really needed the money, I had a man come in to see me from Singer sewing machines. He sat down and said: 'Your job is to get the chumps to come in for the $90 machine and then we'll bring them up to the $200 machine.' I stopped the meeting right there.

"The lipstick guy here learns, though. I love the part when he says, 'Sit down', and Don says, 'No'. You should respect your clients, but there are times when you just have to tell them, 'I don't think you should advertise.'

"When I first came into the business, there were one or two female copywriters [like Peggy]. They wore hats to the office and they were seen as being different and got to work on things like lipstick. But as the world grew up – and you see it happening in Mad Men – women took on a bigger role. At one point I hired more women vice-presidents than any agency including J Walter Thompson and Young & Rubicam which were much bigger. I liked the idea of having women there because they're smarter and they make men better. And in the agency there was sexual tension, so I found that people came to work earlier, stayed later, dressed better and everyone performed better."

1962

Season Two

EPISODE ONE: For Those Who Think Young

"Young people don't know anything." DON

Welcome to February 1962. And the first episode of Mad Men's second season. A year has elapsed in the Mad Men universe. And, as such, we've got questions: What happened to Peggy's baby? Did Betty confront Don with affair suspicions? Has Draper's Don/Dick dual identity come back to haunt him? Is Sal out of the closet? And, most importantly, did Pete ever get published in the Atlantic? As ever we're given more questions than answers.

John F Kennedy is still King of Camelot, Chubby Checker is still on the radio and the Beatles are still a Hamburg club band. The world's changed since we were last in Manhattan, but not that much. The same team remains at Sterling Cooper. Betty and Don are still together. The only things that look vastly different are Peggy Olson's waistline and Kinsey's bearded chin. Oh, and there's a brand new Xerox 914 photocopier causing quite a stir.

In the office, Peggy is now one of the gang of creatives – albeit one who's treated with arrogance and misogyny by the rest of the team. "Air travel's too expensive to waste on your wife," sneers senior copywriter Freddy Rumsen, right in front of her. Peggy's weight loss remains a subject of debate too. Some suggest it was due to Don's lovechild. Pete obliviously reckons she's been to a summer fat farm.

Tonight's episode is themed around youth. Duck reckons clients – perhaps spooked by Doyle Dane Bernbach's VW ads – want fresh blood to sell their products. Don, oblivious to the creative revolution being led by kids in the New York ad world, thinks that "young people don't know anything". He speaks to a few young bucks, but his heart isn't in hiring them. Not that his actions don't spook beardy Kinsey and the other thirtysomething execs.

Although the human drama in Mad Men is stunning, the professional side of life at Sterling Cooper is just as interesting. We started season one looking at Don and co as masters of the advertising universe. Now, as they struggle with a half-baked pitch for an airline, it's more obvious that a company run by an old man, a drunk womaniser and Don (a slightly less drunk womaniser) is beginning to slip behind the zeitgeist. Yes, Peggy's got ideas, but she's still a Sterling Cooper kinda girl. Perhaps some outside-the-box youngsters might kick the place up the backside and see it competing with the DDBs and, in future, the Mary Wellses and Della Femina & Partners.

Betty, meanwhile, is slowly becoming stronger. She's grown in confidence and believes in her own independence. The scene where she flirts her way into a cheap car-repair deal proves unequivocally that the girl who used to live by herself in New York doesn't need her husband to get by.

Is this independence what's saving her marriage? All the women Don has shown an interest in – department store owner Rachel Menken, bohemian illustrator Midge, and Helen Bishop (albeit just a brief flirt in the garden) – are strong independent types, who explicitly don't need Don in their lives. They use him as much as he uses them – unlike Betty, who was almost completely dependent on him. Now, she seems more interested in her horses than being a housewife and oozes confidence because of it. The scene where the two meet at the bottom of the staircase for dinner on Valentine's day suggests the thrill is definitely back in their relationship. Until they drunkenly get to the bedroom.

NOTES

- Is Don's trip to the doctors foreshadowing something? Or just a sign that Draper is as fallible as the rest of us?

- Don removing the hat from the man in the lift was almost as good a scene as Betty taking revenge on the birds.

20TH CENTURY TALES

- After Don's bedroom-failure, he and Betty flick over to NBC and catch Jackie Kennedy in the middle of her guided tour of the refurbished White House, which was watched by 56 million people on Valentine's Day 1962. We also see Sal and his new wife watching it, which answers one of my earlier questions.

CULTURE WATCH

- "Now I am quietly waiting for the catastrophe of my personality to seem beautiful again," Don reads from Frank O'Hara's 1957 poetry collection Meditations In An Emergency. He later posts it to an unknown address.

EPISODE TWO: Flight 1

"There's life and there's work." DON

Last night we joined the young ad execs at a party at Paul Kinsey's pad all the way out Montclair, New Jersey. Kinsey looks debonair with his beard, his cravat and boho mates; the rest of the Sterling Cooper team and their wives look decidedly awkward in such a mixed crowd. As Pete's wife Trudy suggests when she proffers: "I have no problem with Negroes, I'm just worried about the car."

From this, race and racism become a major part of one of the episode's subplots, all set up with an exchange between Joan and Kinsey's black girlfriend Sheila. Some pretty despicable comments from Joan ("I didn't think Paul would be so open-minded") build into a tiff between the ex-lovers that could run and run. Especially as Kinsey took revenge by pinning up a photocopy of Joan's driving licence on the wall so that all and sundry could see her age (32).

The next day at Sterling Cooper, Don and Roger enter the office to see a crowd huddled around the radio. It's not astronaut John Glenn's ticker-tape parade that they're listening to, as Roger suspects, but the news that an American Airlines flight has crashed into Jamaica Bay, just south west of Idlewild Airport.

We later learned that one of the victims was Pete's dad. This leads to an odd scene where Pete goes to proto-father figure Don's office to tell him the news first.

Speaking of Machiavelli, the partners and Duck are using AA Flight One's demise as an opportunity to pitch for the airline's lucrative account, thanks to one of Duck's contacts from London. Don, who's toiled on the smaller Mohawk Airlines account, isn't too thrilled to swap a solid contract for the promise of just a pitch. Especially as he's the one who's going to have to dump Mohawk.

For all his many personal faults, Don is a loyal fellow at work. If you can look beyond his philandering, that is. He seems to crave a solid world to fit around the far-from-solid constructs of his authored identity. So being forced to be so disloyal to the Mohawk chap must have hurt. We'll see how that plays out as the bid for American Airlines rumbles on in future episodes.

We also saw Duck ask Pete to help him try to win the airline pitch using his dead dad as a dealmaker. Pete, almost surprisingly, says no. Then, not at all surprisingly, he turns up at the meeting to offer his help. And his dead dad. It's like an episode of The X Factor.

NOTES

- Christopher Allport, the actor who played Andrew Campbell in season one, actually died in an avalanche January 2008. As such, his death was written into the story.

20TH CENTURY TALES

- Linda McCartney's mother, Louise Linder Eastman, was also on board the real ill-fated Flight 1. It crashed on 1 March 1962.

- The parade in John Glenn's honour was in recognition of the success of the Mercury-Atlas 6 mission which had seen him become the first American to orbit the earth.

CULTURE WATCH

- Peggy's mum is reading Irving Stone's biographical novel about Michelangelo, The Agony and the Ecstasy. A book about the painter is a subtle nudge towards Katherine Olson's deep Catholicism.

THOUGHTS FROM THE TYPING POOL

JoeDoone Considering how Don and Pete got on in the first series, there was something of a rapprochement between them here (good to know that people made tasteless jokes about disasters back in the day, not just now). Until later when Pete comes back, anxious for more of the solace he received earlier, but Don has just had a row with Duck over Duck's ambulance-chasing approach to winning accounts, and Don snarls "This isn't a good time." Pete withdraws, crestfallen. He ends up with Duck and the man from American Airlines. There will be no future rapprochements.

Promethea Don telling Pete "it's what people do" [ie, go home to grieve] seemed like a summation of Don's whole life. He has this whole facade set up (wife, family, suburbs; mistresses, drink, suits) but all of it is just him doing what he thinks other people do … and he's got so good at it he can sell the dream back to them. But he doesn't know why they do it – there's a deadness of feeling in him, after all he's (technically) a dead man.

Sexedup Did anybody else think Pete's storyline was just slightly anvilicious as they say in the US? We realise he's supposed to be a tragic figure, who's at Sterling Cooper for his name, to bring social kudos. But isn't it just too one dimensional to have him repudiating his father, capitalising on him so grossly, by having him use his death to attempt to secure the AA account?

I think Pete is as interesting a character as Don, but to me this feels like character capitulation. Maybe there's a twist in the tale, but I thought the scene played false.

EPISODE THREE: The Benefactor

"A guy like that must know how to make a charming apology, or he'd be dead." ROGER

The Benefactor introduced two fairly minor quandaries into the Sterling Cooper office, namely The Jimmy Barrett Problem and Harry's Wage Dilemma.

First off, Jimmy Barrett – a famous comedian hired by Sterling Cooper – insults the portly wife of the man whose potato chips he's promoting with a stream of weight-related zingers. The Utz contract is suddenly in doubt and the consequences of Barrett's act include: Don sleeping with Barrett's wife, Don sacking his meek secretary and, finally, Don assaulting Jimmy's wife in order to force the comedian into apologising.

When Mrs Barrett tells Don that Jimmy doesn't care about "some glib ad man", we see him whirr into mad man action.

The notion that a slimy comic could push Draper about was pretty laughable anyway, but if we doubted his ability as a fixer before, we definitely don't anymore.

We've seen Don in the role of professional firefighter for Sterling Cooper before (remember him saving the Lucky Strike pitch in the very first episode?) and here he unscrews the pooch with terrifying effect. The most shocking moment of all – the one that has you turning away and thinking "did that really just happen?" – is the moment Don grabs Bobbie Barrett under her skirt in a gesture of desire turned to assault. Remember those moments in The Sopranos when Tony went from gentle giant to an utter horror (the murder of Big Pussy, for example)? Well, Don is obviously no Tony but, after witnessing his near-breakdown at the end of series one and his Valentine sweetness so far this series, for him to suddenly act in a way more befitting a character in a David Peace novel brings his ruthlessness horribly back to the fore.

And his sacking of his secretary Lois who, poor girl, simply tried to cover for him while he was at the movies, was extremely harsh – today it would be industrial tribunal harsh (what wouldn't be at Sterling Cooper?).

The Benefactor's other major plotline involved Harry Crane, who at the opening of the episode is accidentally handed Ken Cosgrove's payslip. Harry opens it, only to find that Ken earns 50 per cent more than him. There's a bit of light relief as media buyer Harry tries to fix the envelope, but the story serves as a nice reminder as to everyone's place in the office. As Sal points out, Harry's salary might be commensurate with his worth to the company:

Sal: "Isn't media a meritocracy?"

Harry: "I've got merit."

The expanding Mad Men world is helping the show to form new layers. Not only are we learning more about the supporting characters, but we're meeting their other halves and understanding their family dynamics. Harry's wife is pregnant and wants to be able to say that her husband is doing well. Harry feels under pressure to feed his family and wants more money – but gets bought off by Roger with the offer of a new title as Head of TV.

Mad Men creator Matthew Weiner explains that this episode is all about what married couples do for each other. It would be glib to disagree with the showrunner but, for me at least, Jon Hamm's performance is so powerful that all you're left thinking about is Don – his flaws and his motivations. For all we've learned about his past as Dick Whitman, his imbibing of Don Draper and his professional voracity, we still know nothing about what really drives him. He's a Gatsby who's got his Daisy and escaped Jay Gatz. So what next?

One final point. As the Drapers drive home from dinner at Lutece, Betty starts to cry. She claims it's because she's so happy at Don letting her into his business life. It sounds like an obvious red herring but, heartbreakingly, I think she was telling the truth – which just goes to show how little Don shares with her. For all Betty's mutual flirtation with Judge Reinhold-lookalike Arthur, her private life has nothing to even compare with her husband's.

NOTES

- Some excellent dry wit from Betty after riding buddy Arthur tells her: "You're so profoundly sad."
  Betty: "No, it's just my people are Nordic."

CULTURE WATCH

- Betty's riding buddy Sara Beth compares hapless rider Arthur to Montgomery Clift's character in A Place in the Sun, a film based on An American Tragedy by Theodore Dreiser. The book's protagonist reinvents himself after accidentally killing a child, before falling in love with both a poor girl and a rich girl – ultimately ending in tragedy. An omen of things to come for Don?

- Patrick Fischler is fantastic as Jimmy Barrett. He seems to be an amalgam of various 50s/60s comics like Don Rickles and Jerry Lewis.

- Is the episode's title a nod to Great Expectations?

- There's a bit of debate on the blogs about what film Don was acutally watching on his afternoon off. I certainly didn't recognise it.

THOUGHTS FROM THE TYPING POOL

Avian Regarding the film Don is watching, at a special Mad Men symposium sponsored by the University of Southern California's School of Cinematic Arts, Matthew Weiner when asked about the movie,

"Its a very rare French film. A film by ... a famous director. I wont tell you the name. I won't say the title. I'll never tell ... because I dont have the rights to it."

It's definitely not La Jette. It could perhaps be an Alain Resnais short?

KeithyD The film was almost certainly Resnais' Last Year At Marienbad. It had been released in the US in March of 1962 and would have been the kind of film that ad men would have gone to see because of its "arty" pedigree. It contained lengthy voice-overs from characters such as the one we hear in the show.

Avian I've seen the wonderful Marienbad many times and I can assure you it's not that film. Though I still feel it could be part of Resnais' oeuvre. Imdb lists the François Villon poem we hear quoted on the soundtrack in the Abel Gance film La Tour de Nesle which ends with a recitation of the aforementioned poem. The film was released in 1955. The only problem is that it was shot in colour. I know it's stretching it a bit, but is it possible Don is watching a black and white print of this movie?

EPISODE FOUR: Three Sundays

"That was beautiful. Are you going to say Grace now?"
KATHERINE OLSON

So far in series two Peggy has been reduced to something of a background character. But here, over the course of three spring Sundays, we learned an awful lot about the Olsons and their odd family dynamic.

The device used by the writers to explore this was the introduction of young, out-of-town preacher, Father John Gill (played by Colin Hanks) who, let's say, reinvigorates Peggy's interest in the church. After Peggy's mum has Father Gill over to dinner, copywriter Peggy helps him out with public-speaking tips for his big sermon, and everything's looking rosy for Ms Olson.

But then we witnessed a moment of hostility from sister Anita, as she told mum Katherine that Peggy is getting away with murder. Katherine, it's fair to say, was nonplussed. Perhaps, because her younger daughter is doing so well professionally, she can turn a blind eye to Peggy's nonchalance.

It's great how the tension between Peggy and her sister has been building up since the start of the series; a glimpse here, a look to the floor there, a snarky comment now and then – but nothing too obvious. It's been hinted at, but finally boiled over with Anita going to confession and telling Father Gill everything about Peggy having given birth to a married man's child and how she hates her sister for it.

It could be read as spitefulness by a sibling envious of her sister's city living (after all, Peggy couldn't have possibly kept both the baby and her job) but you feel for poor Anita. After all, she's the one confined to the house looking after a husband with a bad back and a baby and young child of her own to look after. Meanwhile her sister flirts with the dishy priest and swans off whenever she pleases. Peggy's obviously in a sticky situation, but she's also the one being praised by her mother for her swish job.

This whole plot arc was deftly done. We suspected this confrontation was coming. Using Father Gill to do it, rather than a glass-smashing dinner-table argument, was as subtle and nuanced a trick as you'd expect from the show – a predictable scenario made infinitely more interesting by keeping the protagonists away from each other.

All of this culminated in Father Gill giving Peggy an "I know" Easter egg for the kid at the end of the episode and Peggy doing some quick mental arithmetic to work out if he knows and how he knows. Great stuff.

"My dad beat the hell out of me. All it made me do was fantasise about the day I could murder him." DON

Meanwhile, at the Draper household, Betty's had enough of Don bottling out of disciplining the kids. We meet the pair canoodling in bed on a lazy Sunday morning, only to be interrupted by Bobby and Sally. The kids' innocent naughtiness continued through the episode – a burned hand here, a broken record player there. All to Betty's annoyance and Don's ambivalence.

While Don is a total bastard to the people he works with, and his wife, and his secretary, he's reluctant to be horrible to his kids. He was beaten as a kid and turned out to be a git – a fact he's more than aware of. Is this why he's less likely to be a strict disciplinarian? Or is it, as he says, because he just doesn't want his kids to hate him like he hated his dad.

Ambiguity seeps through everything Draper does. He's been pretty nice all episode … then he goes and throws the robot at the wall, and shoves Betty in the chest. Then, just as we're turning against him again, there's the scene where Bobby apologises and tells Don, "We need to get you a new daddy", which was heartbreaking.

NOTES

- The American Airlines bid failing after Duck's contact gets fired … Don 1 – Duck 0. Also, more proof that Sterling Cooper may not be quite the big hitter Sterling and Cooper might like to think.

- Duck to Harry at the airline meeting: "Why are you here?" Has Harry's promotion gambit failed?

- Poor little Sally, pottering around the office making mischief. Anyone who has had the dubious pleasure of an afternoon at their father's office will appreciate her naughtiness. Dropping gum on the floor, admiring Joan's chest, disturbing Kinsey and, er, getting drunk.

- Is Roger Sterling heading towards a mid-coital heart attack?

- Father Gill dropping Peggy off was the first urban exterior shot of this season. It's obvious why it had to be – Mad Men is shot in a LA studio – but it makes you realise how much of the Mad Men world is indoors.

CULTURE WATCH

- In the last episode at the stables, Arthur talked about his girlfriend and how she reminds him of a character in F Scott Fitzgerald's The Diamond As Big As The Ritz. Here, we briefly see Betty reading Babylon Revisited and Other Stories, a 1960 Fitzgerald collection featuring, yep, The Diamond As Big As The Ritz. Presumably she's interested in more than just Arthur's taste in literature.

THOUGHTS FROM THE TYPING POOL

DellaMirandola I loved the Draper parenting dynamics. Betty wants things to be just like a Norman Rockwell painting; Don is much more aware of the messy realities of life – but then he's also the one who wants Betty to be a window-dressing wife to fulfil his own fantasies of the perfect home. Not since Lydgate and Rosamund in Middlemarch has there been such a portrayal of a marriage so nicely showing how character and social conditioning intertwine.

EPISODE FIVE: The New Girl

"I guess when you try to forget something, you have to forget everything." DON

Perhaps to address the relative sparcity of Pete so far this series, we open The New Girl with Pete and Trudy sitting in a fertility clinic to find out why she can't get pregnant.

Obviously, we know Pete's sperm are in order. What was really interesting here was that, apropos of nothing, when Pete talked about stress, it led him to reveal his insecurities about work ("I'm completely replaceable") to a doctor he hardly knew. He has barely confided in anyone but his reflection before – save an ill-judged attempt to adopt Don as a father figure in Flight 1. I also liked him protesting a bit too much at any suggestion that he's less than a "red-blooded American man".

Later, after Pete finds out from Trudy that it is she, not he, who has a problem, we get another interesting peek into his psyche. First, he's utterly selfish in his reaction; then, we get the distinct impression that Pete is just playing at being a grown-up – talking to his wife the way he thinks "real" men do. This, coupled with the way he overstates his importance to friends and relatives, and the way he's so proud of his building-vaulting sperm, shows him up as a brat. Trudy is right – it's immaturity, rather than vaingloriousness or sneakiness, that's at the heart of his misdemeanours (from Peggy, to Don, to Trudy).

"This is America. Pick a job and become the person who does it." BOBBIE

Don's affair with Bobbie Barratt continued, with some late night, boozey driving leading – somewhat inevitably – to Don crashing his car. What was much more interesting than that was what we learned about Don and Peggy's mutual history.

It was a genuine surprise when Peg turned up with the money at the police station to pay Don's bail, not that he has many other discreet allies. The chance to see Don in front of one of his subordinates without his practised veneer of Draperness was priceless. It was also the first time in a while that someone other than the viewers got to see Don in a weak moment.

While Peggy played nurse to her, Bobbie did a nice job of asking why Peggy was being so kind, and doing so much for her (and Don). We soon found out that Draper saw Peg in her own moment of weakness, too – lying in a hospital bed, delirious from shock at having had a baby.

So they've got dirt, so to speak, on each other. And a tacit agreement that both things "never happened". But that agreement has different meanings for each of them. For Peggy, it means she doesn't want to be treated badly because she knows about Don and Bobbie. But for Don? When he said, "This never happened. You'll be amazed how much this never happened," was he telling her to have the baby adopted, or referring to his own ability to leave a family behind?

NOTES

- The New Girl in question is Don's new secretary, Jane Siegel.

- Matching shot of the episode: A cut from Pete about to provide a sperm sample, to Roger hammering a bat and ball at his desk.

- Nice continuity touch from the props people: Don's packet of fags are crushed flat when he reaches for them after the crash.

- The reveal of Don sitting at Peggy's bed was straight out of the Lost camera-trick playbook.

CULTURE WATCH

- Rachel Menken and hubby are on their way to see Sondheim's A Funny Thing Happened On the Way to the Forum, which opened in May 1962 – meaning four months or so have passed in these first five episodes.

- As Ken tries out his chat-up lines on Jane, Freddy interrupts him – wonderfully – to play Eine Kleine Nachtmusick on his trouser fly: "It's Mozart!" he shouts.

- Don likes Antonioni. Or at least La Notte. Say what you like about him, but the man knows his cinema.

THOUGHTS FROM THE TYPING POOL

ThomasJay I liked that Peggy took some of Bobbie's advice on board and stood up to Don at the end – asking for her money back and calling him Don rather than Mr Draper, seeing him as an equal and not as a superior.

DellaMirandola There are lots of layers and connections at work. Eg, the doctor telling Pete that it's all part of the great circle of life – cut to the circle of life in the office as Joan gets engaged and a new secretary comes in to start flirting with the guys; the connection between Peggy's comment to Don in the car about her forgetting that this happened versus his comment to her to forget things, along with us of course appreciating Don Draper telling her from his own bitter experience "you'll be amazed how much this never happened".

I don't think Pete is immature though, so much as totally conforming himself externally to what society expects of him – but having bouts of articulating his dissatisfaction with that. Thus, yes, he was a git to Trudy but also the only one who's questioning – in his case *"Why* have a baby – just because that's the next thing we do now we're married?" Compare Don not really questioning whether to sleep with Bobbie, or Joan not really questioning the triumph of a ring on her finger. Pete and Peggy are the obnoxious ones, but they're also the ones who are questioning the mores of the society around them – the questions that the "me generation" of the 1960s did ask. This series does a good job of showing the good and the bad of that nascent revolution.

Horatio93 [On Joan's appearing one-dimensional so far] The Glory and the Tragedy of Miss Holloway's life is that she can not change. Not outlook, not ambition, not style. That is why the driving licence on the notice board was so devasting – time marches on past her, but she will always believe her life reached its apogee at, say 26.

EPISODE SIX: Maidenform

"Women want to see themselves the way men see them."
PAUL

Peggy's established herself as an important voice at the company. She knows she's better than Pete, and when he tries to gazump her with his "Thanks, Clearasil" sell she's just as quick to put him in his place: "It's all about keeping your father-in-law happy, you do your job and I'll do mine." *Translation:* You're only here because of who you are.

Despite this, Peg is still having to scrap for territory. The boys come up with a new sell for Playtex while enjoying a sleazy night out at a bar. In the meeting, Peg lets go the fact that she's been bypassed and copes admirably, too, when the boys say she's not a Jackie or Marilyn but a Gertrude Stein. They're right though, she is no Jackie or Marilyn because she refuses to be categorised by their male world. She's also not afraid to tell Freddy exactly what she thinks about not being involved. It's hard to watch, especially when Cosgrove literally closes a door in her face.

To counter this, she has something of an Olivia Newton-John at the end of Grease, vamping up and joining the boys at the Tom Tom strip club. She's doing what she thinks she has to – to be central to ideas at Sterling Cooper but, by taking Joan's advice ("Stop dressing like a little girl"), is she kowtowing to the restraints of the era, or just using the last page of the playbook to make sure she's not overlooked at work? Either way, she's not happy. As Elisabeth Moss says in a video accompanying this episode on the AMC website, "she knows she'll never be one of the boys". But she's ready to mix it up to get what she wants. Good for her.

"I know you're not good in the afternoons." PAULINE PHILLIPS

Head of Accounts Duck Phillips has been central in this year's office-based storylines, but has remained something of a curiosity. In Maidenform we found out that he's divorced, his ex-wife is remarrying an old pal and planning to dump the family dog on him and he had a drink problem. "I know you're not good in the afternoons," his former wife kindly tells us/him.

Duck's also still reeling at the fact that Don's got an "I told you so" to hit him back with (American Airlines). He's struggling with sobriety, too, as you can imagine anyone with a drink problem working in the booze'n'fags-drenched environs of Sterling Cooper would be. It's this craving for a drink to wipe the stress away that leads to poor Chauncey's demise. The dog's withering look as Duck contemplates the scotch is heartbreaking. But Duck deals with it by frogmarching Chauncey downstairs and ditching him in the murky Manhattan streets.

NOTES

- Don's creative conservatism is shown again – witness him defending a decade-old campaign, plus all the American Airlines nonsense.

- I loved Pete mugging to his brother about how important he is to the company – "My absence is felt." He also uses this import to seduce a Playtex model and accompany her back, oh dear, to her mother's apartment.

- Despite his many flaws, Roger's handling of the Don/Duck feud showed some excellent managerial skills

- Note the Utz crisps on the fridge during Don's existential moment back at the house – the ghost of Jimmy Barrett?

- Goofy Freddy seems to represent the idea of a competent white middle-aged man who hangs around long enough to drift into a senior role. He may have spotted Peggy, our diamond in the rough – but you can see that the likes of him won't last for much longer.

20TH CENTURY TALES

- Betty's friend at the country club casually describes the weather as being like "the summer they executed the Rosenbergs". Remember "Ethel Rosenberg pink" in series one? Sylvia Plath's The Bell Jar begins by telling us "It was a queer, sultry summer, the summer they executed the Rosenbergs, and I didn't know what I was doing in New York."

CULTURE WATCH

- There was a rare bit of non-period music (possibly the first non-diegetic bit of music in the series, too) as the Decemberists' The Infanta (from their wonderful 2005 album Picaresque) soundtracked the ladies and their various dressing routines at the top of the show.

- Duck makes the series' second reference to A Funny Thing Happened On The Way To The Forum. Like Rachel Menken, Duck's kids have already seen it.

- Pete childishly ruins The Man Who Shot Liberty Valance for Peggy. She doesn't rise to the bait.

THOUGHTS FROM THE TYPING POOL

Bella79 The way they flicked between how men view women in general, and then how Don views the specific women in his life was breath-taking. As was Don's sudden, horrific realisation of what he is doing and how it is starting to affect his daughter. Sally's look of hero-worship at the club when she looked at her War Hero daddy was beautiful.

DellaMirandola Peggy wearing pantyhose ties in with her querying the idea that all women want to be Jackie or Marilyn: they're not a sexy garment, they're functional. She's not dressing for male approval there, she's dressing for herself. Though I'd say at the end of the episode, she's not dressing for male approval either, she's dressing so that she can network with the boys at the strip club.

AlexJones My main observation was the dramatic irony of them choosing Marilyn and Jackie Kennedy as the two opposing models for women and then having to shelve the campaign "for a couple of years" – by which time Marilyn will be dead and Jackie will be a widow. (And of course we all know, as they presumably don't, that JFK was allegedly having an affair with Marilyn.)

Insomniac506 It's wonderful watching Duck's quiet downward spiral. It's clear that his drinking destroyed his marriage – his wife's passive-aggressive comments are her final nail in the coffin of their relationship – but instead of leaving us with the well-worn cliché of a man alone with his dog, Mad Men's writers up-end expectations and have him throw the damn thing out the door. What perfect casting of dog to match owner, too – a big melancholy looking shaggy thing who mopes around self-pityingly, as Duck does himself.

Horatio93 Duck is simply a cipher – Don's antagonist, the only competition or threat Don faces in the office. Roger was emasculated by the stair-race and heart attack. Pete only managed to widdle on the great man's shoes. What is more subtle is that the *real* danger Pete and Duck pose to Don is not professional but psychic. They represent the Ghost of Draper Past in season one and of Draper Yet to Come in season two.

Season one was about Don's secret past; the callow youngster Don/Pete (and I can imagine Pete would also piss himself when under fire) tries to steal the identity of the older mentor Don, both metaphorically in the workplace, and literally by stealing the photographs. The threat of exposure triggers very real panic in Don, and Pete nearly succeeded in driving Don out of his own life.

I suspect season two is to some extent about the dangers of Don's future, the consequences. Indeed the very first scene was Don's physical exam, the lifestyle is killing him.

As Pete is an image of what Don was, Duck is a ghost of what he might become, an alcoholic, thrown out of the home by his wife, estranged from his son and daughter, separated from the dog he gave them.

CrossYourHeart My dad worked in the 60s for several agencies mentioned in the series, and travelled to the US frequently. He was also a marketing director in Playtex, so he could have been at the Sterling Cooper pitch. The rejection on grounds of over-sophistication of the Jackie/Marilyn campaign, in favour of price and fit, is spot on for that company: I roadtested their sample bras. I also remember the dinner interviews for which my mum had to dress up in appropriate cocktail wear, to satisfy the US bosses that she was the right sort of wife. Do the writers have a mole or what?

Meet the cast

VINCENT KARTHEISER (PETE CAMPBELL)
the man behind Sterling Cooper's most conflicted young man...

JOHN PATTERSON

It doesn't take long to figure out that Vincent Kartheiser has been an actor almost all his life. For the hour that I spend with him, Kartheiser, 29 years old and acting for a good 24 of them, is on show. That's not to say he's showing off, but with a ready-made audience comprising myself, a photographer and a PR, he leads us on a merry dance around his Hollywood neighbourhood, talking up a storm, alternating moments of profound thoughtfulness and emotional engagement with silly voices, a lot of rolling eye-play, gossip, good jokes, impolitic thoughts about his neighbours ("I hate this guy's dog, man. It does these human-sized shits outside my house!"), one wicked Malcolm McDowell imitation ("time for some spatchka, me little droogies!"), and then issuing surprisingly wise observations on subjects ranging from loneliness as a central theme in American art to the drinking habits of Scientologists and growing up on stage.

That perilous suspension between youth and experience is a hallmark of Pete Campbell of Sterling Cooper, Vincent's role in Mad Men. Nominally perceived as the villain, especially after his failed attempt in season one to blackmail his mysterious creative director Don Draper – the self-made, working-class alpha to Pete's to-the-manor-born omega – for a promotion and for his unwitting impregnation of Elisabeth Moss's Peggy, Pete has been deepened, sweetened and rendered more complex during season two. Pretty, round-faced, callow and thin-skinned, but with a Manhattan aristocrat's devious, bred-in-the-bone survival instinct, Pete bubbles with entitlement, snobbery and ambition, yet at heart he's the insecure, despised scion of a faded, old-money family with a demanding father who depises his son's career.

Pete is hard enough to like; Kartheiser once described talking about him as "like apologising for a very touchy cousin ... he's unaware sometimes, and he speaks before he thinks." Does Vincent Kartheiser actually like Pete Campbell?

"You know, I feel protective of him. I do that pre-emptive thing where I insult him before anyone else gets the chance to, just in conversation. I was real skinny when I was a kid, so I'd make fun of that before anyone else could. Now I meet people who say, 'Oh, you're that Pete Campbell.' I'm like, 'Yeah, I'm the asshole!' before they can say it. If I have a couple of drinks in me I can get real protective, real passionate! But I love Pete Campbell! I think he's a real fucking character, a real person and Matthew [Weiner] does that – he writes real characters. And he writes Pete Campbell for me."

Kartheiser is out of uniform today, a long way from the tightly tailored, mostly blue period suits that Campbell wears. He's dressed simply in jeans, a long, thin, striped scarf that functions as a useful comic prop in his more antic moments and a shirt that would look ridiculous on anyone else, but suits his model good looks to a T. The essence of Campbell – bulkier and exponentially more uptight beside the slender and laid-back Kartheiser – feels utterly absent today, except for traces of a more likable arrogance and self-confidence that Weiner has shaped and turned to the character's advantage.

Kartheiser owns a house in Hollywood, on a block that seems frozen in the middle of gentrification. His house and several others are immaculately restored or security-fenced, while others are wrecks.

"Sleazy – that's why I love it … I remember West Hollywood and Los Feliz in the mid-90s [two winded old neighbourhoods that later became trendy], they weren't at all like they are now. That's why I want this neighbourhood to change – so I can make money on selling my house!

"You like this house? You wanna buy it? Six hundred and fifty grand sound all right to you?"

He lives a simple life, without a lot of possessions, apparently (we never actually enter the house, so he could be making this all up). "People must wonder when they come to my house," he says. "But I don't have a car, I don't have any furniture, or a TV. I'm not trying to welcome people into my life!"

He's too busy for that, he says. In fact, today he has already done two auditions. Anything good? "Aaaaahhhh," he exhales. "I can't really say. One of them I didn't even get a script, just my sides. Top Secret, like a Woody Allen movie or something!"

Surprisingly for an actor his age, Kartheiser makes few of the kind of career-transforming, attention-grabbing moves – or movies – that you'd expect. He's lucky, he says, because he actually loves acting itself, not the whole brouhaha that comes along with it.

"I started on the stage, man. I did Shakespeare and everything else. I was a kid, so I'd be a page in Henry IV or Henry V. I was Tiny Tim, things like that, national roadshow tours, long runs. Then when I was 15 I came out here and started all this. I'd like to say it built discipline and character and this serious work ethic, but I've always just really liked acting, so it never seemed to me like any kind of sacrifice at all. But I was careful, too. When I was a kid I didn't want to be known in the public eye too much, but I worked a lot."

So he'd probably rather not be famous?

"Well, that's a choice I made. I chose not to audition for some projects or pursue certain agendas I could have when I was about 15. Instead I got to sit back and have faith that good things would happen. Because I just love acting. I didn't at all mind the idea of going to auditions every day. I knew I liked this. I wasn't that worried about cashing out."

We circle back to the house after a photo session in a local park. I asked him to do the "Pete Campbell look", a furious jutting of the jaw and bulging of the eyes. He does it. "You can't really see it with the beard, though. It's all in the chin, the double chin that the collar is pushing up. It changes my whole face wearing those 60s clothes. It's like a disguise. When I have my long hair and when I've got my big old beard going, no one ever recognises me! I really like disappearing, being in movies and people not even knowing I'm in them."

I ask him about loneliness, emptiness and restlessness (as in De Tocqueville's question, "Why are Americans so restless in the midst of such great prosperity?") as the real themes of Mad Men – not sexism or smoking or bullet-brassieres.

"Absolutely. All the men want to be Don Draper, all the women want to fuck him. Everyone thinks he's the perfect man, and Pete Campbell is jealous of him. But Draper's completely incomplete, completely lonely, completely detached, completely alone. It's why he reaches out to all these women, it's why he needs to take charge in business, to belittle Pete. He's completely alone. Loneliness isn't a phase or a mood, it's a core condition of being and some of us deal with it better than others – build a family or make a million dollars. Or Draper, coming home to the empty house at the end of season one. That's a big theme of the show: unattachment, loneliness, distance."

We part. I tell him he's on the gold-standard show on American television right now.

"It makes me happy when I hear that but then I realise I don't know what it means. But then again, you spend your life doing lots of things that no one even knows about, so it's cool."

EPISODE SEVEN: The Gold Violin

"You know what I like about you? Nothing." JIMMY

Don Draper's been as aggressive as he's been enigmatic in season two. We meet him here dithering as to whether to cure his existential angst by fulfilling (originating?) the mid-life crisis cliche of buying a swish new Cadillac. This scene quickly morphed into a flashback of a hitherto unknown part of the Draper story – the years between the war and when we met him at Sterling Cooper in 1960. Turns out he was a used-car salesmen before he was a fur factory copywriter. One supposes the leap to the world of advertising wasn't huge.

What was vital was the appearance of a woman looking for the real Don Draper (ie not Dick Whitman). An ex perhaps? The scene cut as soon as she revealed she knew Don wasn't the real Don, but it does pose a few important questions. We know that Dick's family think he's dead; where on earth do the real Don's family and friends think he is? Did the fake Don spend the years between Korea and Sterling Cooper on the run from the other Don's past? Is he still running?

The look on Don's face when confronted by the woman from real Don's life is almost identical to the look on his face when Jimmy Barrett confronts him about sleeping with Bobbie here at the party – initial confusion followed by the whirring of his brain as he works out how to lie his way out of an ugly situation.

The damage here has been done, though. Betty may have dismissed Jimmy's suggestion that he was being cuckolded – but she *knows* he's right and that all her worst suspicions about her husband are correct.

When Jimmy dismisses Don as garbage, he articulates everything Don knows and thinks about himself. But to hear it from someone else, a man who hardly knows him, must hurt. Not as much as that discussion with Betty when it comes, though. For now she leaves him with the task of having to clear her vomit up from the car.

"So how did you end up in accounts?" SAL

The other focal point of the episode is the conflicted designer Salvatore. Sal's inner turmoil over his sexuality has been overlooked since his "date" in season one. What we have learned, though, is that Sal repressed his feelings enough to marry Kitty and then, last night, that Sal is a bit in love with Ken Cosgrove.

Dropping out of leftfield as it did, the crush on Ken felt slightly heavy-handed. Sal's struggle with his own sexuality, at a point in history when mainstream acceptance of homosexuality was still years – if not decades – away, is a fascinating subplot of the series – especially in the macho world of Sterling Cooper. So, while Sal pocketing Ken's lighter and clutching it while he watches TV felt was tender and sad, the real drama was at the dinner table: namely, in Kitty's face, as she was first excluded and shushed out of the conversation in favour of office minutiae and, second, realised the look in her husband's face wasn't one of professional interest, but genuine longing. She *knows*. And the exchange after Cosgrove left, where Sal apologised profusely, suggested he knows she knows. It's an uneasy truce. Kitty, like so many wives of Sterling Cooper, is trapped in a marriage of status, but of potentially intense unhappiness.

Mad Men is especially good at making its characters nuanced icons of the various social upheavals taking place in the early 60s. So, while Sal doesn't represent gay life in 1962, his is one of the last generations (in New York at least) where homosexuality was an identity to be so ruthlessly repressed. Ditto Peggy. She isn't quite a feminist, but she represents the great moves forward by women in the 60s and 70s. Which, for everyone who wasn't a Gloria Steinem, is probably more representative of how things actually were.

"It's idealistic? That's nice." DON

The youth-led cultural and creative revolution of the 60s is represented by Kurt and Smitty, the two young bucks hired early in this series to take Sterling Cooper from being a Bobby Darrin kind of office to more of a Bobby Dylan one. They returned last night to work on the Martinson's coffee account – ultimately sealing it with a Hawaiian jingle for the brew.

The pair tell Don their generation are sick of being told what to do; they just want to *be*. Don's response – "You just want to be selling Martinson's coffee?" – notes the irony of using the counterculture to sell consumer goods, foreshadowing the future amalgamation into the mainstream of most of those idealistic boomer types. Even Bobby Dylan ended up, like Don, flogging Cadillacs.

New secretary Jane Siegel is the other wing of Sterling Cooper's vanguard of youth. Unperturbed by the Cult of Joan, Jane is happy to lead the other execs by their trousers into Cooper's office to look at his new Mark Rothko painting. She's not afraid to bat her eyelids at Roger (who can never resist a flutter) and, most of all, she's not afraid to stand up to Joan: "Why are you the only one allowed to have fun?" she asks. She's the other side of Peggy Olson's coin – another former Draper secretary. Unlike our Peg, however, she knows how to dress and how to use her looks to get her own way (look at the way she makes Ken feel like a schoolboy). She's not as smart as Peggy, but who knows where she'll end up in the topsy-turvy world of Sterling Cooper?

NOTES

- The Don flashbacks made me realise that his whole backstory is very similar to The Simpsons episode, The Principal And The Pauper, in which Seymour Skinner is revealed as an imposter who took on the personality of his superior officer and mentor in the Vietnam war.

- Did Betty mean Jewish people or showbiz people when she dismissed Jimmy as "you people"?

20TH CENTURY TALES

- There was another tiny subplot running through last night's episode. We had a few of the SC execs thinking of ways to market the relatively new disposable Pampers. Throwaway nappies are just one of thousands of consumer goods marketed in the mid-20th century whose convenience trumped their terrible environmental impact. The writers go back to this later with the picnic scene, in which Don lobs a can into the field and Betty leaves all the picnic rubbish on the ground. The long lingering shot made sure we didn't miss the Drapers' (and thus an entire generation's) laissez-faire attitude to littering and the environment.

CULTURE WATCH

- This week the main cultural focus was the Rothko painting hanging in Bert Cooper's office. As well as proving a stumbling block for Harry in his meeting with Cooper, the Rothko provided a nice prism through which to see the characters: prep school huckster Ken talked about it being "so deep you could fall into it"; Harry couldn't get over the $10k price tag; Jane dismissed it as smudges and squares; Sal was familiar with Rothko but unsure of the deeper meaning; and Kinsey was too cowardly to look. For all the other characters' insight (or lack thereof), it's canny Cooper who's got the painting's card marked. He might have deeper feelings about it (perhaps he realises the link between the spiritual emptiness of some of Rothko's work and the world of advertising), but to him it's primarily an investment, one that could make his family very wealthy indeed.

THOUGHTS FROM THE TYPING POOL

HerrDobbler And of course, the climax of the episode sees Jimmy calling Don "garbage" – neatly finishing off the littering theme. Were they littering Utz packets?

LEA3012 The littering was funny and I kind of interpreted the trash blemishing the beautiful countryside as a metaphor for the Draper family. As they all relaxed out on the grass, they appeared to be the perfect picture, but there is a big black cloud hanging over it all.

CaptainLego Jimmy also seemed uncertain [about what Betty meant by "you people"] but his reply – "comedians?" was spot on funny. The activity around the Rothko was funny, but it was Harry who won out with his honesty and who was rewarded in turn by Cooper's admission that he'd bought it only as an investment.

DellaMirandola Loved Ken being at the same time the most appreciative of the painting (he's a sensitive writer) and the most unaware of everything going on around him (he's a lightweight good-looker who doesn't get that Jane really has no interest in him because she's gunning for much higher game, aka Roger).

Insomniac506 Betty's vomit was perfection – both funny and disturbing. I love the way that she's so repressed that her body has to do the talking (or screaming) for her – first the shakey hands, then the spew in Don's perfect car. Mad Men is very good at feeding us these perfect Norman Rockwell images of Don and Betty's family life and then subverting them. My favourite was when the whole family were laughing on the bed, and then their son broke the bed by jumping up and down, and Betty sent them away. Betty wants to live inside that magazine cover image, but it just won't work, because it isn't real. She's both complicit in the myth making, and its victim, as she has to follow rules she had nothing to do with setting up.

Digit This [Don being introduced to the top table of power by Bert in this episode] is really where the critique is sharpening up. We all think we're too slick to fall for advertising's lies, but that's because we're only spotting the obvious ones. The ones we're missing are the ones that don't look like advertising – like "philanthropy", silkily and sickeningly revealed by Bertram Cooper to be the quickest route to power. I love how this dovetails with the Rothko painting subplot, how he finally admits with a wink that he has it because he expects to double his money on it. Eight years later, Rothko committed suicide while the likes of Cooper carried on clinking cocktail glasses and watching the graphs rise. The veneer of culture, its kindnesses and its aesthetics, are being stripped back to reveal the death's head: it's all a lie.

Mad Men In The 21st Century

As Mad Men's cult appeal grew, its fans on social-networking site Twitter invented online alter-egos for Peggy, Pete and even the noisy Xerox machine

ANNA PICKARD

It's an eternal struggle for bosses around the globe: should you let your employees use the internet or not? In the case of Sterling Cooper, one of New York's finest advertising agencies, it seems they inadvisedly said yes – after all, the wayward employees that make up the cast of characters on Mad Men are literally all over the web. They love it.

Mad Men's obsession is quite remarkable for a bunch of analogue people – especially ones who don't actually exist. While the act of writing a Twitter update might not be remarkable at all, the fact that they're in 1962 makes it really quite impressive.

Last summer, season two of Mad Men started running on America's AMC network, and people noticed the characters starting to pop up on the social networking service Twitter, filling people in on the minutiae of their day. Things like what fictional Madison Avenue meetings they were having; or what fictional lunch they were having with other fictional characters. They even messaged each other – about work, or what time they might be home for dinner – all without breaking character. It was a social network that filled in the gaps around the lives seen on screen.

Devout Twitterers started to take notice. They spotted Don Draper, ad executive and lead character. They followed his silently suffering wife, Betty; they marvelled at spunky assistant Peggy's perfectly in-character musings. Most fans of the show thought it was a subtle marketing push on behalf of the show's producers, a little Easter egg for devotees. After all, it certainly wouldn't be the first time that a TV show has reached into the internet to try and grab hold of readers like an octopus with extra-long digitally manipulated digits. Shows like Skins, Lost and Battlestar Galactica take care to engage and cultivate their online audiences, titbits trickling down from the producers to the fans.

And in this hypermarketed, viral-PR world – where anything interesting online has a crowd of weasels in suits running just behind it with a notepad and rubber gloves, trying to figure out how they can make it poo money – who can blame them for thinking that the Mad Men phenomenon was a piece of in-house guff? Except it wasn't.

In fact, the entire enterprise was just some really, really zealous fans trying to get inside the minds of the employees of Sterling Cooper. Because being a fictional character shouldn't be an impediment to one's ability to waste time on the internet. These people loved Mad Men, and they wanted to drag the characters they loved into their world. By last autumn there were at least 75 different Twitter accounts purporting to be Mad Men characters, including multiples. It started with Don. Then there are at least four Betty Drapers, one of whom has a blog describing daily life in the Draper household, including recipes scanned and tested from authentic copies of 1962 Life magazine.

Last time I checked, there were five Peggy Olsons. That includes BadPeggyOlson, who only speaks her naughty thoughts and another who – as a young ambitious career woman – has made her profile available on the professional networking site LinkedIn.

It wasn't just the central characters, either. The Switchboard has a Twitter account, detailing the thoughts of all the switchboard girls. The Drapers' kids, Sally and Bobby, both have a couple each. Best of all, the office photocopier has a Twitter account. That's right: the photocopier. It's a Xerox 914, apparently, with deep insights into the world of Sterling Cooper: things like "Warming up for a big day of copies, lots of staff memos", and other pithy paperrelated matter.

Things were going well for Mad Men's Twitter citizens' army until, last August, lawyers at AMC got wind of what was going on. Believing there was a breach of copyright here, they got Twitter to suspend the accounts of "Don Draper" and his cohorts. Within a week, however, the accounts returned after the show's marketing department had stepped in to persuade AMC that, whatever the legal standing, it was insane to stop this outpouring of (completely free, you fools) fan-promotion. The makeshift cast of Madmenites revelled in their victory, though the question remained: why were they bothering in the first place?

The internet has long been a home of all kinds of fan fiction – remixes written by enthusiastic groupies. Most of the time it tends towards "slashfic" – stories that inevitably end with the main characters biffing, regardless of gender, sexual preference, interplanetary abode or possession of human genitalia.

For these fans, however, it seemed to be about neither the scifi nor the sex. The fantasies being indulged were ones about being slick, handsome and naturally witty in an era where gender roles were more well-defined, martinis at lunchtime were almost mandatory and smoking didn't kill you – at least not officially.

But there are plenty of TV shows with devoted fans. What was it about this bunch that made them cross over? Perhaps it's partly the fact that so much of Mad Men is inferred, bottled up and unsaid. Smouldering looks and pained glances transmit the things that dare not be spoken out loud. And, frankly, that's not good enough for a modern audience.

Trying to work out subtext is a purely hypothetical concern when you're used to having Facebook updates, texts, blogs and status messages alerting you to every sandwich choice and bowel movement of everyone you know. We're not that used to things going unsaid any more. We don't like subtext: we like subtitles. And if the show's writers weren't going to fill in the blanks, the fans would have to do it for them – with attitude. With Twitter. And with the whole rest of the internet at their disposal.

Google WWDDD and you'll find a whole lot of people fantasising about how life would be much more fun if they could answer every life situation by asking What Would Don Draper Do? In fact, he's got a whole Agony Uncle blog.

To explain how he felt, one Twitterer – the office mailroom boy Bud (actually a marketing strategist in the 2000s, though still called Bud) – put up a site called We Are Sterling Cooper which gathers together some of the feeds and offers a manifesto for fan-created content: "We're your biggest fans, your die-hard proponents, and when your show gets cancelled we'll be among the first to pass around the petition. Talk to us. Befriend us. Engage us. But please, don't treat us like criminals."

Perhaps it's time for TV's bigwigs to realise there's a new fandom out there: devotees who not only reach out to their favourite characters, but want to crawl under their skin – be they philanderer or photocopier.

The last word on the subject, however, surely belongs to Xerox914, who said, on 17 January at 9.52am precisely: "There are still donuts from last week if anyone wants one".

Brilliant. Thanks

EPISODE EIGHT: A Night To Remember

"I'm not even allowed to choose where I sit." BETTY

A Night To Remember is an episode wrapped around the descent of the Drapers' marriage. But, this being Mad Men, where the obvious is as rare as Don's steak, there's a half-hour delayed drop before the drama of last week's confrontation with Jimmy Barrett is brought up (Betty angrily smashing a chair aside). First, there's an elaborate dinner party at Casa Draper for Duck, Sterling, a mutual friend from Rogers and Cowan called Crab, and their wives.

So when Betty finally did snap, it wasn't solely because of what Jimmy said, it was the beers. Having placed Heineken in A&P supermarkets in upmarket suburbs like the Drapers', Don guessed correctly that his own wife would be susceptible to his little marketing push. And, right on cue, at the dinner party Betty proved that "perfect" housewives like her would see the green bottles of Heineken and fall for their exotic style – "Holland is Paris".

Betty, unaware that she was the lab rat in Don's calculations, was unamused ("What an *interesting* experiment"). She knows

Don was giving her shrink backhanders. She knows how much he dominates her emotionally. She knows that her bucolic surburban lifestyle is turning her into a wreck. So, for Don to use a dinner party that she'd spent a whole day making (along with the redoubtable Carla) this was the last straw. The beer test may have seemed trivial to Don, but for Betty it was a pivotal moment. Without it hammering home what little psychological respect he has for his wife, she might never have had the guts to confront him about Bobbie.

Their initial argument is hand-over-mouth fraught. Betty literally couldn't understand why Don would subvert their "perfect" (Duck's words – it must seem perfect to him) world with Jimmy's wife: "How could you? She's so *old*." She's so completely submitted herself to this Stepfordian world, to this Betty Crocker persona, that she can't fathom why he would stray from it – we see this when she later asks, quite honestly: "Do you hate me, Don?"

It's rare that Betty holds the cards in their relationship but, as she accuses him, she's in charge for once. Don, a man almost unmatched in his ability to lie, can hardly deny it. The Draper doth protest too little. And yet, he will not confess. He'll keep on breaking poor Betty Hofstadt's pretty little heart.

The next 24 hours, in which Betty, unchanged from her dinner dress, skulks around the house looking for evidence of Don's misdemeanours with only a glass of burgundy for company, is heartbreakingly sad; you can see the collision between doubt and anger wriggling around January Jones's forehead – as the makeup wears off, so do her illusions. Everything she's ever thought she had to be has been ripped up from under her. The foundation of her marriage is as strong as her three-legged marital bed.

Brilliantly, the moment where she finally stands up to Don and tells him to stay away from the house is inspired by Jimmy Barrett's (so we thought) irrelevant Utz advert from episode three: "Am I crazy? I don't think so," whistles Jimmy at Betty as she glances at the ad on TV. Poor Betty doesn't think so either, and that lands Don a hot date with the breakroom couch. Ouch.

"It's Madison Avenue." PEGGY

Meanwhile, Father Gill's reappearance last night provided the audience with another look at Brookyln Peggy Olson. BPO, as opposed to NYPO, is the Manhattan high-flyer. In her meetings with Father Gill and the ladies from the church ball, she's the cool kid for the first time in her life. It's her calling the shots, playing the Draper role. She's confident, she knows what she's doing and she's not going to let Gill use the church to cow her.

Is Father Gill interested in her because he knows about the baby and is worried for her spiritual wellbeing? Wanting her to confess to him and move on with her life? Is he just keen to befriend a young person rather than middle-aged ladies desperate to feed him? Or is he simply attracted to her?

Regardless, Gill is desperate to coax Peggy's guilt from her. His speech when he meets her in the office seems one of concern, rather than church busybodying. Peggy's response to his "God already knows, whatever it is," was "Well, then I don't need to talk." Which shut him up.

The thing is though, she does need to talk. If not to John the singing priest then to whom?

"Get your department in line or I'll gut it." DUCK

Harry Crane's jobbing role as head of TV has so far provided a few neat comic asides. But the department's burgeoning workload, and cockup on the Maytag/communism front, gave Joan an opportunity to prove that she's more than the dethroned queen of office totty.

Joan's been happy to push her boobs up against the glass ceiling so far. There have been few hints that she wanted to do a Peggy. So last night, it was especially sad to see her find a real niche at SC only to find the glass ceiling staring right back at her (as usual), as the genuinely decent, but bumbling, Harry managed to completely miss the fact that she's brilliant. Idiot.

Joan being gazumped by Jane, and seemingly content at home with her doctor fiance, who we met last night, has obviously given her pause for thought about what she's doing with her life and her career.

The fact that Harry had managed, in effect, to demote himself proved he's not hardy enough for office realpolitik. He and Joan would have made a heck of a team.

The episode finished with a final montage of everyone undressing at the end of the day, providing a nice bookend to the fired-up dressing scene at the beginning of Maidenform. Joan's got a sore shoulder from her bra strap: she's literally been pulled down by her own figure. Peggy looks like a corpse sat sullenly in the bath, and Don, not for the first time, is left alone, staring into the abyss. The only person who looks happy is John "Zimmerman" Gill, who whips off his dog collar, pulls out his guitar and starts shredding some Robert Johnson … sorry, some Peter, Paul and Mary. An excellent, if unexpected, end to proceedings.

NOTES

- Poor Peggy pretends to be her own secretary when Father Gill rang.

- Some zoological introductions from a smirking Roger at the party:"Crab, Duck. Duck, Crab."

- Don and Duck have become quite team. As Horatio93 pointed out in a previous episode's comments, they're more similar than Don would like to think.

- Pete on seeing Father Gill in the office: "Did we get Miracle Whip?"

- Ken understands the importance of juniors: "You need someone to lay down on the barbed wire so you can run over them."

- Pete's "Where's *my* invitation?" face when he learns about the Drapers' dinner party was brilliant.

- Betty Draper's International Smörgåsbord in full: Gazpacho from Spain, a hors d'oeuvre of rumaki "from Japan", a leg of lamb from Dutchess County, mint jelly, egg noodles the way Grandma Hofstadt made them in Germany. With a choice of burgundy or Dutch beer.

CULTURE WATCH

- Peggy's ailing brother-in-law likes high sea tales such as Hornblower but – "I was right, there's only one book about Moby Dick," Peggy informs sister Anita.

- The show Betty was watching with the kids was Make Room for Daddy (aka The Danny Thomas Show – a Mad Men favourite). Something Betty clearly wasn't prepared to do.

- The Peter, Paul and Mary song that Gill sings is Early In The Morning.

THOUGHTS FROM THE TYPING POOL

DellaMirandola I'm not usually a fan of Joan Holloway, but that cut from Joan being transmuted from Joan the hip script-reader to Joan the demure water-fetching housewife, to Betty at the dinner party was fantastic. Joan, this is where the life that you think you want leads – but is it too late to do anything about it? Again a great piece of acting with her eyes in the scene where Harry tells her that they've got this obviously substandard guy in to do the "real" job. Oh, and her fiance is a lightweight schmuck. Why, Joan, why?

Insomniac506 The episode belonged to Joan. There've long been clues that, despite her perkiness and apparent ease with being the office hottie ("I've never wanted your job", she told Peggy blithely a few episodes ago), there's much, much more frustrated ambition just below that gorgeously bosomed surface. She's ten times more capable and personable than Harry Crane, the ultimate fumbling, incompetent pen-pusher, who passes her over without even noticing. Again, she's trapped by the limited roles men have constructed for her. Sterling's comment to Crane about Joan being distracted from her "other" duties reveals that to him, she's just some nice office candy for him to ogle.

Digit How really genius of this show to suddenly open such depths of feeling in a character [Joan] who's seemed driven by nothing but shrewd expediency, and to do it with such devastating economy: "It's a hoot", she chirped gamely to justify her new field of activity. And you just know what she really wanted to be able to say was "This is the first really interesting thing I've ever done and I've suddenly got such *hopes*..."

Also, Peggy writes the line "A night to remember" [for the church dance], while doggedly trying to forget her night with Pete. Talk about the return of the repressed.

DellaMirandola I like that you can't box Father Gill into your usual priest-in-a-drama box. Does he fancy Peggy? Probably. Is he sufficiently a good priest not to act on that attraction, other than to try to keep pulling her back to the church? Also probably. He served in this episode the function of telling us that there is no clear line between old and new school. He believes in the traditional church – but when he's alone in his room, he doesn't wear a hair shirt but dresses like James Dean and plays hip folk music.

PaulMacinnes It's a funny (modern!) place we find ourself in where a product, Heineken, has – most probably – paid a significant sum of money to be placed prominently in a drama during which it is used solely as a means of humiliating a heroine and as a dirty consolation to our disgraced hero when forced into exile. Wonder what Joan would advise the client to do if she read a script like that ...

RiverAngel This is a corruscating critique of patriarchy. The women have to stay loveable to their masters, whether it be their husbands, their senior work colleagues or God (all male). Father Gill's questioning whether Peggy thinks God can love her is so loaded with this and his song, all about Judgement absolutely sums this up. This series isn't just about who fancies who, that's just the small stuff. As a work of fiction, Mad Men does more for the justification of feminism than a hundred women's studies papers.

EPISODE NINE: Six Months' Leave

"Some people just hide in plain sight." HOLLIS

It's August in Manhattan and Marilyn Monroe is dead. Thank goodness those Playtex ads never made it through the net. Apart from Peggy (neither a Jackie or Marilyn be), most of the office girls are in tears – even cool Joan had to take a lie down.

Peggy's comments in the lift to Don and Hollis are obviously pertinent – all of the Mad Men and women hide in plain sight after all – but, as well as this, Monroe, whose perfect exterior hid inner turmoil, is a canny reference point for the outwardly immaculate Don and Betty.

The main issue in the office was Freddy Rumsen – who'd drunk himself into a state, wet his pants and flaked on a meeting with Samsonite before squelching off home. Pete, who's happy to blame Fred, then takes the credit for Peggy dealing with it, tells Duck who tells Roger who fires the long-serving, but pretty useless Freddy.

This being Sterling Cooper, Roger's idea of sending Fred off to dry out involves taking him out for drinks. And then more drinks in a speakeasy-style underground casino for the rich and famous, before sending him off into the abyss. "If I don't go into that office every day, who am I?" asks Freddy before he gets into the cab. The high, almost brutal, turnaround in staff is a key point in Jerry Della Femina's book. Is Freddy to be the first casualty of many?

Fred's leaving drinks culminated in Don meeting Jimmy Barrett in the speakeasy and sucker punching the cuckolded comedian for ruining his marriage. Which, if anything, is a little bit unfair on Jimmy. But, as Roger said, it's probably not the first time he's been punched. Was Jimmy's "look, it's The Man in the Gray Flannel Suit" a metatextual reference to the book/movie Mad Men is so often compared to, or just an acknowledgement that even the characters in the Mad Men narrative world realise Draper's similarity to Tom Rath?

"Two coronaries ... You have to move forward." ROGER

Roger's affair with Jane was a complete surprise. There were hints in the Rothko episode and various references to Roger's disillusionment with his marriage throughout both series – but Roger's philandered before and never left Mona. It seems surprising that he would have such a seemingly intense affair with Joan but never leave his wife and then trot off with Jane after what, a few weeks? Also, was it not a bit odd that Roger told Mona what Don said at the bar and used that as justification for his actions. A year and a half after being nursed back to health by his distraught wife too. Regardless, the Joanification of Jane continues.

"I got my diagnosis the other day. I'm bored." SARA BETH

Back upstate, Betty was still trying to figure it all out. She defrosted the freezer and lined the drawers to regain some normality but, before long, the wine glass was back out and she was trying to break into Don's drawers. Is there a chance she'll find something about Dick Whitman rather than Bobbie?

In the end, after talking to Sara Beth – who's under the impression that Don is still "perfect" – she entertained her own desires vicariously by setting up Arthur and Sara Beth on a lunch date, cannily taking the phone off the hook to avoid the consequences. She's not quite got the guts to have an affair yet – why not watch how Sara Beth copes?

It's creepy behaviour. And, as if that wasn't clear, the next scene had Don castigating Ken, Kinsey and Harry for laughing at Freddy with the line: "Don't you have anything better to do than dine on the drama of other people's lives like a bunch of teenage girls?"

This episode felt like a real pincer between the development of the first portion of the series and the conclusions soon to be drawn. And what about Peggy honorably taking her promotion? That glass ceiling's getting weaker and weaker.

NOTES

- Peggy was right about Playtex. Looks like she's even copying Don's luck.

- Don's now on his fifth secretary in two and a half years.

- Roger's story about an ex-alcoholic colleague: "He only drinks beer now."

- The shirts Jane buys Don are from Menken's.

- "There's a line, Freddy – and you wet it."

- Is Don keen on keeping the likes of Fred because it makes him look better?

- Freddy on Duck: "He's as dry as a bone – he doesn't understand this business."

20TH CENTURY TALES

- The boxer in the bar that Don, Roger and Freddy visit is heavyweight champion Floyd Patterson.

CULTURE WATCH

- Betty is reading Ship of Fools by Katherine Anne Porter – a 1962 bestseller that satirised the origins of Nazism and painted a bleak picture of the human condition. You presume it won't provide a pick me up.

- Sara Beth says she can't wear long gloves anymore "after Gypsy" in reference to the Sondheim musical and film about burlesque dancer Gypsy Rose Lee.

THOUGHTS FROM THE TYPING POOL

RoyHudd It seems that Don Draper is still stuck on Rachel. When he, Roger and Freddy were trying to get into that gambling den, the pseudonym he chose was Tilden Katz – Rachel's new husband. So even when his marriage is in meltdown and he's pickled, it's Rachel who pops into his head first. [There's a real Tilden Katz, an old college buddy of Matthew Weiner].

JoeDoone That's the second time that Mad Men has referenced Tom Rath; in the first series, Don came off the elevator, and Roger looked him up and down and said: "Very Man In The Gray Flannel Suit."

LEA3012 In terms of Marilyn's death, you might not have expected Joan to be so soft hearted. But this is about what the death of the Marilyn image means to her. We've established that the women of America were either a Jackie or a Marilyn (!) and as Sterling so delicately pointed out Joan was certainly more of a Marilyn. At a time where she is struggling with her identity, here she is symbolically witnessing the death of it.

Insomniac506 Pete had a small but priceless moment of venal self-serving Peteness. When he mentioned that a client had just

had a baby, and Sal queenily pitched in with "A boy or a girl?",
Pete, who clearly has no genuine interest in other peoples' new
children, assumes Sal has suggested this as a line to impress the
client. Genius writing. Pete would be monstrous if he wasn't
such a gimlet-eyed little beta-male.

Oldmuskrat This episode had something of a Freudian "couch"
motif recurring: people lying down on the couch and others
walking in on them (or not). Like Joan after hearing the news of
Marilyn's death (the long shot of her in the velvety darkness
looked like she was lying in state); poor Freddy waking up from
the couch after wetting himself; a semi-sozzled Betty waking up
on the settee from a face down on cushion position (perhaps an
echo of the same position that MM's body was found in?); Pete
sneaking 40 winks in his office (he thinks he's power-napping, of
course) when Peggy storms in and finally Don characteristically
having a nap in office time as Mona bursts in to confront him
about Roger's betrayal.

Insomniac506 The couch thing is fascinating. We know that all
the characters are desperately in need of therapy, but apart
from Betty and her bored housewife friend (who was diagnosed
as "bored" by her doctor), everyone is resisting it like crazy. Yet
there they are, all scrunched up on their own little couches,
isolated and vulnerable, like children. It's like each of them are
longing to return to the womb.

DellaMirandola I loved that Roger seemed such a good guy all
episode (in the scene with Joan, in managing the Freddy
situation, and in his chat with Don at the bar) only for it to be
revealed that all of this has resulted in his caddish decision to
leave Mona. All his talk to Freddy of new beginnings, his talk to
Don with that line Mona flung in Don's face – it was all serving
his decision to throw away his own past for Jane whom we all
know doesn't really deserve it. Though this is another of the
moments when we see the old-fashioned '50s versus new and

strange 60s divide. Is it really better that Roger remains adulterous but respectable, or that he decide to make a break and marry the new woman?

RiverAngel The exposure of Roger's affair with Jane was a clever touch in an episode all about exposure vs deceit. It resounded against the key phrase from Hollis, "Some people hide in plain sight".

Betty Draper's Feminine Mystique

To see the existential confusion of Mad Men's disconsolate housewife is to grasp the relevance of The Feminine Mystique

LIONEL SHRIVER

Betty Draper has everything a woman in the early 1960s could possibly want: a handsome high-earner husband, an attractive suburban house, rambunctious kids, and a clatter of pleasant distractions – horse-riding, children's birthday parties, coffee klatches. Shy, demure, and terribly pretty, this waif has embraced what Betty Friedan would soon christen "the feminine mystique": a life of stay-at-home bliss, ferrying her kids to the dentist, finding a new lampshade for the den that matches the curtains, dressing to the nines for her husband's ad-agency dinners. Betty Draper presents a vision of exactly what postwar American women were encouraged to regard as the perfect life.

Yet something is wrong. Betty lies awake at night. She drinks during the day. A petulant furrow mars her lovely brow, and she's afflicted with uneasiness, mournfulness, disquiet. In an effort to resolve her aimless, elusive dissatisfaction, she sees a psychiatrist – who doesn't listen. He needn't. He's seen so many women like Betty before.

When she wrote The Feminine Mystique in 1963, Friedan was herself living in the suburbs and raising her children. The results of a questionnaire she sent to graduates of her Ivy League women's college surprised her. Though most of her classmates had gone on to similar lives as gratuitously well-educated housewives, they didn't seem happy. Thus Friedan set out to describe why the exclusively wife-and-mother role prescribed as the postwar feminine ideal was a dangerously comfortable trap. In her groundbreaking work – re-issued in Britain in March 2010 – she encouraged women to enter higher education and pursue serious careers.

Yet these days, in both the US and the UK, more women enrol in universities than men. The term "career girl" long ago lost its frigid, arid stigma; working women in the west are now the norm. So has The Feminine Mystique mouldered to mere historical artefact?

Of course, there's nothing "mere" about this book, which not only recorded history, but changed it. If we now take it for granted that capable women get university educations, have careers, and earn their own incomes, that's in significant measure due to Betty Friedan. She challenged the assumption that females are necessarily homebodies, who find their true contentment in polishing furniture, sauteing corned-beef hash, and wiping runny noses. Not that long ago any woman who found this shut-in role unsatisfying was regarded as having something wrong with her. So the very seeming irrelevance of Friedan's text today is a tribute to its radical effect.

Nevertheless, women are still paid less on average than men, often for the same work. They remain underrepresented in management positions and still assume a disproportionate share of housekeeping and childcare. Selling women products based on unachievable idealisations of what it means to be female is still going great guns, from diet drinks to anti-ageing creams to plastic surgery. Scan the world leaders at a G20 summit, the current US Congress, or today's British parliament and count the female faces (don't worry – it won't take you long).

Even in the sexual arena, the constricting morality of the 1950s has been replaced by the default assumption that, unless you can come up with a good reason not to, you do it. The virtual obligation to put out on just about any date borders on a new slavery. For unattached women, to go from having to sleep with no one to having to sleep with everyone constitutes a dubious form of freedom.

Granted, Friedan may have placed excessive faith in work, not always a privilege. Manning the checkout till at Iceland can be every bit as monotonous and soul-destroying as scrubbing the kitchen floor. For many women today, a job is a joyless fiscal necessity. For a woman who does thankless cold-calling for telemarketers, baking her family a plum tart at the weekend may provide one of her few creative outlets.

Hence the recent emergence of women keen to restore the role of housewife and mother as a legitimate, defensible life choice. Fair enough, should her partner willingly assume the breadwinning burden, any contemporary woman can still embrace the feminine mystique. But in that case Friedan's warnings are as germane today as they were 50 years ago: go in with your eyes open.

Spoiled but mysteriously disconsolate, Betty Draper is exiled from the world that we career women now inhabit. With the division of labour in the household so stark, she has little real comprehension of what her husband gets up to on Madison Avenue. She loves her children, but she's lonely, unfocused, and tortured by existential confusion about what, exactly, all this ostensibly blissful domesticity is in the service of. So any woman seriously considering the new "freedom" to choose housewifery and motherhood as a substitute for a demanding career should watch every episode of Mad Men back to back, perusing the re-issue of The Feminine Mystique during the adverts.

Why I love Betty Draper

POLLY VERNON

The pre-emptive, knowing chatter on series two of AMC's extraordinary Mad Men confused me. This time, said anyone who knew anything about high-end, thoughtful, exquisitely styled and elegantly scripted American dramas, it's All About the Women. I thought this was odd. As far as I was concerned, it had only ever been about the women. But *tant mieux*, I reasoned, bring it on. More exposure to these staggering creations could only be good for my soul.

The gals of Mad Men are fabulous, without exception. They are the anti-Mistresses. They are nuanced and contradictory, surprising and bad. They are at least a little bit mental, and they are never anything less than inspirationally well dressed. Or half-cut, for that matter. But I only worship at the shrine of one of them. (Anything else would be exhausting, no?) I love office manager Joan Holloway, of course. I loved her from episode one, series one. I love her skin and her sardonic smoking style and her instinctive scheming. She is pure sex in a scarlet woollen day dress; and she is the least vulnerable of all the characters, which makes her something of a relief in the grand scheme of their myriad miseries.

But this far into series two, it's Betty Draper – Betsy, Bets! – who's inspiring all the breathless devotion in me. It's Betty D whom I worship. Partly, sure, it's because of the way she looks. It is her glacial, Kennedy-woman-standard gorgeousness, it's the flick in her eye liner and the gloss on her hair. Plus, her costumes are stellar. I dream of doing equestrian chic as well as Bets; I cannot pretend I haven't channelled the jodhpurs and cream-crew-neck combo, because I have.

Beyond this, though, it is her absurdly complicated character that's ensnared me. No character makes less sense than Bets. No one's agenda is more opaque. No one's motives are more scrambled. No one's end game is more obscure. And yet, and yet – no one is more plausible. I don't know precisely why Betty Draper went into her backyard and shot at her neighbour's birds in episode nine of series one – and yet, I get it! I totally get it! I do!

Series two, and Betty is effectively shooting at doves in her every scene. Episode one: she offers the call-out mechanic a tiny bit of sex in return for roadside rescue, and I loved it. Episode two: she makes a fellow horse-riding student fall in love with her in the most calculated fashion imaginable, and then she cries because it was all a little too easy and too frightening in the end. And I loved it. Episode three: she flirts with her husband's obnoxious comedian client, ostensibly to keep him on side, but actually because she needs to be fancied by every man, all the time. And I loved it. I love each of the thousand tiny ways Betty Draper finds to rebel against her philandering, dissatisfied husband – without even realising this is what she's doing.

EPISODE TEN: The Inheritance

"The hardest part is realising you're in charge." HELEN BISHOP

Parenting provided neat bookends through various points of The Inheritance's plot, from Harry's baby shower, to Pete and Trudy's adoption saga, to Helen and Betty's single motherhood right through to Betty's father's illness.

Betty's father Gene has had a stroke, and not for the first time – something both we and Betty find out after her father's girlfriend neglected to tell her. This gives Betty cause enough to let Don back into her world temporarily in order to keep face for a trip back to her parents' home.

Betty's been marginalised by her stepmother, made to feel guilty for living out of state by her brother, and her dad – John McCain-lookalike Ryan Cutrona – keeps forgetting who she is. It's a family all right, but there's no warmth there at all – she's left out of things here like she's left out of her own life by Don. Gene's post-stroke confusion manifested itself with him confusing his daughter and his dead wife, resulting in the evening's first inappropriate touch as he groped Betty.

Gene, despite his castigation of Don ("He has no people, you can't trust a person like that"), is obviously adored by his daughter. He's a strict type – he used to fine the kids for small talk – and probably the kind of authoritarian man about the house that she wishes Don was. That's a world Betty understands, not the ambiguous world of the early 1960s. As she does with old maid Viola, Betty crumbles back into being a little girl around Gene – for him to be so far gone is another spoke removed from Betty's fragile mental wheel.

Another character struggling with his parents is Pete Campbell, whose mother chastises him for wanting to adopt a baby (even though he doesn't) and for letting Bud deal with their father's estate. Like Betty, Pete balances on the precipice between adult and child – tonight, he appeared to have forgotten which side he's on, as he gets drunk at the party and, in the way Bobby Draper might brag to his daddy, told Peggy: "I'm going away … on a plane."

Pete's gabbled conversation with Peggy involves telling her, off the cuff, that he hates his mother, as if this is normal talk in the repressed confines of Sterling Cooper. Why on earth would he say that, we think, before realising he's drunk. His childlike self-regard is made glaringly obvious by his snipe at Peggy – he sees nothing beyond her rise – "Everything's so easy for you."

We then cut from manchild Pete to childman Glen Bishop. Glen's been camping out in Sally and Bobby's toy house in the garden after running away from mum Helen and her new boyfriend. He's come because he still sees a kindred spirit in Betty.

This is the first time we've seen Glen since the oddities of their relationship in 1960. Wise beyond his years, but still, essentially, just a 12-year-old kid, he's come to rescue Betty from her suburban prison. "I've got money," he assures her as they watch cartoons together. Glen sees something in Betty – she's pretty, kind and lonely – and Betty sees some of the same in him. It was sad to see the inevitable and Betty facing his wrath for calling his mum. If only she had a husband as devoted to her as young Glen.

These scenes were all about the confusion between the psyche of the adult and child. Betty's a little girl when hugging maid Viola and telling her to look after her daddy; Glen is obviously confused about his own state of development – one minute he's holding Betty's hand, the next playing trains with Bobby and Sally; and Pete's being picked on by his mother one second and putting the kibosh on Trudy's attempts at motherhood the next. They're all half grown up, half grown down. The Inheritance of the title isn't the gaudy ceramic that Betty's sister-in-law took – it's being our parents' children.

Before we move on, a quick point on Betty and Helen's chat. She's the first person she's told about Don leaving (or so we know), having moved quickly from admonishing Helen's parenting skills to realising that she could soon be in the same boat. "Sometimes I think I'd float away if Don isn't holding me down," she whispers.

"Please Hollis, it's Paul." PAUL

It was nice to see the subplot of Kinsey and his girlfriend Sheila return last night. We discovered that Paul had made a promise to join her in travelling to Mississippi on a Freedom Ride. We also learned that despite all his talk in the van travelling down there ("consumer has no colour"), he was much happier with the idea of going to an aerospace convention in California than actually going through with pushing the Civil Rights cause.

His facade of of liberalism was once more scratched when lift operator Hollis greeted him as "Mr Kinsey" (as he usually does, presumably), and Kinsey, in front of Sheila, made a point of telling him to call him Paul, despite probably having never acknowledged him before. Hollis, who works in a building full of bullshitters, knows one when he sees one.

Not that Kinsey is completely full of it. Far from it, I'm sure he's genuinely in love with Sheila and cares about the Civil Rights movement. It's just that his heart clearly lies in advertising. That horrible little line – "you can go and work in any supermarket" – says more than any admirable activism could. But maybe we should cut him some slack – he does go south after all, even if the brave choice was his second choice.

NOTES

- Now that smoking in pubs looks weird on TV, and smoking in the workplace is positively antique, Don smoking on the plane at the end looked absolutely bizarre.

- Pete had his big-day blue suit out for both visiting his mum and the plane ride. His reaction to Trudy's adoption plans is to literally bury his head under the covers.

- Roger and Jane are already at the giving shared gifts stage of their relationship. Tiffany's gifts, too.

- "Who knows what he does or why he does it? I know more about the kid who fixes my damn car." Gene Hofstadt's got Don's number.

CULTURE WATCH

- Pete refers to Alfred Hitchcock's 1948 Rope when he jokes with his brother about killing his mother.

- The two comics of Glen's that Betty picks up are an Action Comics with Superman on the cover (later alluded to in the exchange between Betty and the boy) and Metal Men. Metal Men being shapeshifting robots with artificial intelligence created in 1962.

THOUGHTS FROM THE TYPING POOL

Insomniac506 Did anyone else feel the temperature drop when Roger walked into Don's office? Joan all but shrivelled up in her skin whenever Roger spoke, and Don dealt with Roger more like a demanding child than his boss. Add to that the casually snide comment someone made about Roger and Joan being together, and it's clear that Roger's stock is way down in the firm, and he's now officially a joke.

And, vicious though it was, I loved Joan's complete belittling of Kinsey in front of the whole team ("You'll need to return your tickets and name badge immediately"). She's been waiting for a moment to pay him back [since he pinned her age on the break room wall].

I was intrigued by Pete's wild-eyed, sinister reference to Rope, about two prep school boys (Leopold & Loeb) who try to commit "the perfect murder". Pete seems to have an attraction to films involving alpha male psychopaths – remember when Trudy referred to him watching Cape Fear compulsively a few episodes ago?

DellaMirandola "Remember Rope?" was the best line of the episode. You could almost believe that Pete and his brother have spent hours planning how to kill their mother.

UncleSchnorbitz Joe Meek's Telstar leads us into the end credits.

Not only is it a seminal piece of music from the Mad Men era but it also ties in neatly with the storyline. The tune itself celebrates the launch of the eponymous communications satellite that would have a wider influence on shaping the advertising world in the years to come. In addition, this space age song accompanies Don on his journey to the space age conference.

LEA3012 There was also a little theme of finding comfort or a confidante where you least expect it. Don and Betty's midnight mischief [at her father's house]; Pete's conversation with Peggy; Betty and Helen Bishop and of course Betty and Glen. Pete seems to be getting snowed under by all the conflict and responsibility of his marriage and is turning again to Peggy. Apart from their conversation, notice his little look when she hands him the cake.

Bedelia Betty's desire to regress to a childlike state is set against her realisation that she seems perpetually trapped in a sexual role for all the men in her life – she has used this to get what she wants in the past (in modeling, in bagging Don, in being the Grace Kelly Queen Bee of their set), but now realises that it's an empty kind of power. She seduces Don at her dad's house, because it's comforting to her at the time and boosts her self-confidence to know that she can still have him eating out of her hand, but she makes the point that she's in charge – it doesn't mean anything.

DellaMirandola I do love these moments where Pete, who tries so hard to tell everyone exactly what he thinks the rules say he should tell them, suddenly comes out with his real and strange feelings to Peggy. After all the pretences about parenthood in this episode (note even that according to the Laws of Manly Office Banter, Harry isn't allowed to find anything positive in being a father, he's supposed to lament the fact that he won't be getting any from his wife for a while), Pete's long-overdue outburst of honesty was actually a relief. As with Betty, there are lots of crumbling facades in this series – we're starting to see some walls actually come down.

PhelimONeill Another great Pete moment when he suggested they take back the donation his father had made. He really has no idea how the human race works. He almost seems glad that he hates his mother as it, in his eyes, makes him appear interesting. His comment about going on a plane seemed to be all about his passing drunken befuddlement at not feeling anything at such a clearly significant event.

MissBean Glen's "I've got money" line to Betty was the same thing Don said to Rachel Menken when he tried to run away with her in the first series? What does it say about Don that he uses the same lines a young boy would. He's running away to California just like he wanted to in that episode as well.

EPISODE ELEVEN: The Jet Set

"Why would you deny yourself something you want?"
JOY

We first meet Don here in LA in his grey flannel suit at the side of the pool. Surely even *he* can't be that cool. We soon found out that TWA had misplaced his luggage and he was stuck in his "Don Draper" costume.

Pete – wearing his "lucky" blue suit – was desperate for a swim but Don reckons their time would be better used schmoozing clients before the conference proper. Not long after, having first seen a Betty lookalike, Don was approached by Viscount Monteforte d'Alsace and his ladies, asking Don to join them for dinner.

With Pete preoccupied by seeing Tony Curtis ("Don, a thing like that!"), talk of the end of the world at the arms presentation encouraged Don to follow his libido and take Joy's (Joy!) offer of a trip to Palm Springs. Would he stay and talk shop with Pete – or disappear with the girl? Tough one.

We then had some odd scenes with Don mixing with Joy and the rootless Monteforte jet set at a Californian mansion. "Who *are* these people?" wonders Don on behalf of the audience about the ragtag bunch of old-money Eurotrash. They're trotting the globe living out a sexually and economically liberal lifestyle – they're like Midge's pals from series one, but with a boat in the harbour at Monaco. Hanging with the rootless, beautiful rich. Isn't this Don's fantasy?

Sort of, here he fits in and out but shows up his poor background when he mentions money and his football playing days – before redeeming himself with his knowledge in the name-the-city game. But even he was a bit spooked out when he discovered that the Viscount was Joy's father. Combined with the arrival of a man with his two children, this appeared to have kick-started Don back into the real world. We next saw him on the phone, presumably ringing Betty and the kids, but introducing himself as Dick Whitman. Who is he speaking to?

His relationship with 21-year-old Joy provided a neat mirror to Roger's with Jane. Both men's power is teetering – Roger is about to get shafted by Mona, Don's about to get shafted by Duck (who's scheming to arrange a Sterling Cooper merger) – they're making wahey while the sun still shines.

A quick note on Don's collapse – the first scene of this series suggested that Don's health would be a major theme. It hasn't so far, so when he collapsed with heat exhaustion at the side of the pool I presumed it would be more serious than it was. As it was, it was just another layer of his master of the universe veneer peeled back. If he felt ill now, just wait until he gets back to Duck's anschluss of Sterling Cooper.

"If you have a man that you'd like to go to the concert with tonight, I completely understand." PEGGY

Back in the office, beside Duck engineering a merger with PPL, Roger and Jane's intense relationship and Kinsey's travails down south, the main plot point was the tremor of a date between Peggy and Kurt, to see Bob Dylan. But, poor Peggy, just as she's getting excited, Kurt outs himself in the office, to the fratboy jeers of Harry and Ken and the arched eyebrow of Sal.

This news was obviously no big deal to Kurt's pal Smitty, or even to Ken and Harry, who despite their horrible sneering seemed over it by the time Pete returned. The elephant in the room though was Sal. He froze when Kurt told them he was gay, a generation or two too late to blithely reveal a detail that's eating away at him.

Peggy, meanwhile, has chosen the wrong boy again. But this time it does at least feel like she's the master of her own destiny – the staff defer to her now and it was her who approached Kurt – she just needs to find the right chap. The Draperisation of Peggy continued too with the Right Guard campaign – she's adamant that their existing campaign is worthwhile – much like Don is/was with Playtex.

The Jet Set hints of transatlantic cultural clashes. The difference in attitudes between the nomadic Monteforte horde and the missing suitcase that is Don Draper; the difference in openness between Kurt and Sal; the impending culture clash that Duck's trying to engineer between his employers and perspective buyers PPL. It's been 17 years since the war and 15 since the Marshall Plan – Europe might not mean what it used to for the likes of Don and Roger for much longer.

NOTES

- Sal casually thumbs a Playboy in the Right Guard meeting.

- Duck's back off the wagon? Was tonight his first drink?

- Some beautiful direction by Phil Abraham in the weapons

presentation. The spooky shot following Jon Hamm's face as he collapsed was great too.

- Don's never eaten Mexican food.
- Duck gets a case of Tanqueray gin, ie, it's English, ie, it's from Powell, ie, deal on.

20TH CENTURY TALES

- They're watching black student James H Meredith go to university in Mississippi, an event that caused race riots killing two and injuring 75. Is that Kinsey in the crowd? (No.)

STERLING COOPER SPEAK

Ken: (After Kurt announces that he's homosexual) "I don't think that means what you think it means."

Harry: (On the Oxford riots) "I don't know why people keep stirring up trouble, it's bad for business."

Cooper: (On negotiations) "Let them open the kimono."

CULTURE WATCH

- It's only been a matter of time before Bob Dylan was mentioned explicitly in Mad Men. Unsurprisingly it's young Kurt, who's been to see him play Carnegie Hall.

- Pembroke College dropout Joy is reading William Faulkner's The Sound and the Fury. It's "just OK", apparently. It won't be when she discovers the last page is ripped out.

- Johnny Mathis sings What'll I Do? over the closing credits as Don is far away from his wife and family.

THOUGHTS FROM THE TYPING POOL

Bella79 The "Dick Whitman" line absolutely threw me. I can't think of a single character we've met yet who would know the truth, but also to the level of saying "Dick Whitman" as opposed to simply "Dick". Did this tie very neatly in with Betty's Dad's comment last week about Don not having any people? He does. And now we're going to meet them. Also, isn't the Cuban Missile Crisis due soon? If so, lovely build up with the arms race (and lovely comparison of Pete's eager enthusiasm and Don's growing fear during the presentation).

Oldmuskrat When Don becomes part of the rich poolside set it was a bit like a cheesy version of that Pasolini movie Theorem where a mysterious stranger (played by Terence Stamp) enters a bourgeois household and seduces everyone then leaves. Not that Don goes *that* far but I bet the old Viscount wouldn't mind if he tried. Don has a fainting fit by the pool and when he revives he wisely refuses the sinister "medicinal injection" from the resident Dr Feelgood. Was that a reference to Max Jacobson, the fashionable quack who used to give amphetamine injections to JFK et al?

Insomniac506 The episode was about the appeal of transformation, and of living another version of your life. Obviously Don has been doing this already, as he expertly fractures his life into compartments. He gets to play with the idle rich, another variant on his affair with Midge, but on a much grander, yacht-owning scale. Flirting with the Viscount and his daughter represents the ultimate departure from responsibility, the chance to disappear from his life. It's continually fascinating to watch the way in which he simultaneously is and isn't within his own skin, and how he's both an insider and outsider in every social situation he's in.

And of course, being Don, it's all about the power dynamic – mostly, he wants to dominate and conquer every situation he's in, but sometimes, like last night's episode, he's happy to be seduced (literally) into following along with the Glamazons. There was something so fun and trashy and Valley of the Dolls-ish about the Eurotrash jet-set he was hanging out with, which is fed as much by Don's love of 1960s European cinema as anything else.

DellaMirandola Totally disagree that that the episode is about transatlanticism. Surely the key is in Roger's line about "this is the life I was meant to lead" and Joy's line to Don about "you should have what you desire" (not an exact quote). In this episode we see two sides of the "new" 60s mentality – go for what you want, don't pretend to conform and sneak what you want in on the side. Roger's side ("no, honestly, I was miserable with Mona") shows us the negative – the way self-fulfilment can lead to self-centred choices that hurt other people. So in a way does Don's. Meanwhile Kurt and Peggy showed us the positive side: it can't be regretted that Kurt feels he can pursue *his* sexual desires without pretending to be straight; on a lesser level Peggy isn't, Joan-like, getting the ersatz freedom of a date every night, she's getting the freedom to make the most of herself and go out without it needing to be a date. And most powerfully of all, the James Meredith enrolment at Ole Miss story.

I keep making the Middlemarch comparison, and here Duck's strengths and weaknesses are leading him Bulstrode-like down a path he and Roger may both end up regretting. I love the way Duck becomes the rainmaker with killer instinct that Cooper says he hired him for only by losing what he was trying to re-invent when he moved to SC – the drunken man who lost his family tried to become the sober father and has failed dismally. What does it profit a man if he gains the chairmanship of SC and loses his own soul?

Insomniac506 In the scene with Roger and his lawyer, Roger mentions "I'll send Mona to Reno". This was a common strategy employed by spouses who wanted quickie divorces. One spouse would go to Reno to speed up the divorce hearing (with its famously liberal divorce laws) and presumably also escape the social humiliation while it was all going on. Claire Luce Booth's play The Women, made into a film by George Cukor, has the heroine going to a divorcee's ranch in Reno to wait out her divorce from her husband.

KeithyD I'm surprised no one has yet mentioned The Great Gatsby as a probable influence on Don's character. Like Gatsby (Jay Gatz), Don has changed his name and has attempted to deny his past in order to create a new persona. Gatsby was also said "to have killed a man" and fought in a war. His parents were farm people from the Mid west. But unlike Gatsby, Don has found and held on to his Daisy – though the state of their marriage might well reflect how Gatsby's marriage to Daisy would have turned out, what with his ability to dissimulate and keep secrets.

This plays into one of those American myths – the ability of Americans to recreate themselves as who they want to be. Don's confrontation with the Europeans forces him to confront his real identity (hence the call as Dick Whitman at the end – a name incidentally that echoes Dick Diver, another Fitzgerald character seduced and then repulsed by Europeans, and Walt Whitman, whose line "I sing the body electric" could have been written about Don.) Don is a late-century Gatsby, trying to create a self that "works" in his environment while concealing the real self of which he's ashamed. In this era it's advertising, not running booze. He is truly following the American dream as it appeared at that time.

Incidentally, the last two pages of The Sound and the Fury show Benjy – who has learning disabilities – beginning to bawl and cry out (the sound and fury, signifying nothing) because the cart in which he's been taken through town takes a left turn besides a monument instead of a right one. His brother is able to calm him by turning the cart to the right so that Benjy sees the houses and the road pass by each "in its ordered place" (the last lines of the book). This isn't crucial to understanding The Sound and the Fury, but what it does do is show the roots of Benjy's frequent panic attacks – things have to be in the right order, done in the right way. Perhaps we can relate this to Don's need to have things done in his way. Though if the last page of the book is ripped out, perhaps it's a sign of him at last abandoning order and going with the 1960s flow.

EPISODE TWELVE: The Mountain King

"So, there'll be another Mrs Draper?" ANNA

The person who Don, as Dick Whitman, rang at the end of The Jet Set was Anna Draper. The real Don Draper's widow.

What was more surprising was that as well as giving Don tacit approval to "be" Don, she's now his only link to his real past. We see from his interactions with her, both in the 1962 present and in flashbacks, that around Anna he could literally be himself: admitting his mistakes to her, telling her things he's never told Betty. We learn that, in return for subsidising her career as a piano teacher/cutlery-windchime-maker on the Californian coast, Anna was quite happy for Dick Whitman to assume her deceased husband's identity. Even being so generous as to grant him a divorce as a Christmas present.

The juxtaposition between Dick and Don was made clear enough by Draper's clothes. He arrived in his trademark grey suit, but, for the second time in a few episodes, Don was handed a bag of new clothes by a woman who wasn't his wife. The last time Jane gave him a top-up to his Don uniform – new clothes from Menken's. This time Anna went to Californian department store The Broadway to get Don some casual slacks – the kind of clothes you might wear while admiring a '34 sedan and thinking of the easy life in the west. You can't help but feel he'd be happier just sacking it all off and moving here with Anna. He still doesn't know who he's supposed to be: "I have been watching my life. It's right there. I've been scratching at it trying to get into it, but I can't."

Beside Don's continuing adventures in the Golden State, last night saw developments for many of the Sterling Cooper family: Roger and Bert approved the sale of the company to PPL; Kinsey returned from the south having been dumped by Sheila three days in (she did well to last that long); Betty's weird vicarious puppeteering with Sara Beth and Arthur took an odd turn as she turned from confidante to moraliser and Pete's dagger of Damacles finally dropped – he still won't adopt and thus his father-in-law pulls the lucrative Clearasil account. His throwing the turkey out of the window was wonderfully, quintessentially Campbell. But one has to respect him for letting the account go rather than be bullied into having a child he didn't want.

"Why don't you just put on Draper's pants while you're at it?" PAUL

Peggy, as always, was a bit of a star in this episode. Leading the Virgin Mary-styled Popsicle campaign with Draperesque aplomb, bagging Freddy's plum office and swaggering about drinking and smoking. Her contrast to Joan was, more than ever, stark. From the start of the show the two have been – though de facto allies – established as opposites, representatives of different sensibilities. They're envious of each other too. Peggy of Joan's confidence and her charming (we thought) fiance; Joan of Peggy's careerist bent and freedom – though she does seem quite proud of Peggy's ascent.

Joan must be envious of Peggy for slightly darker reasons too. Peg's not the one stuck with Dr Greg, whose Mr Hyde side emerges here. After we'd seen him rebuff Joan's advances in their shared bed – he chose a quiet moment in Don's office to rape a shocked Joan. This removal from the perfect life Joan had led herself to believe in was certainly the most shocking moment in Mad Men so far – Christina Hendricks's resigned look to the drinks cabinet utterly chilling as the camera panned away.

The writing hinted at the fact that Greg has some serious issues with Joan's sexual past – he admitted to feeling inexperienced while they were in bed and sniffed at Roger's familiarity with Joan. This sexual loathing seemed to out itself in that compulsive sexual assault. Marital rape wasn't a crime at this point – but they aren't married yet. Even so, there'll be no repercussions for Greg, you fear. Where on earth does Joan go from here?

"The Catholic church knows how to sell things." PEGGY

Christianity oozes through The Mountain King. Sal kicked off the theme by mentioning his mother sharing out Popsicles like a priest breaking bread, Peggy ran with it, developing the Virgin Mary as dispenser of ice snacks ad image ("The mom looks familiar," mused Mr Popsicle), and Matt Weiner finished it off with the final scene of Don baptising himself in the Pacific over the music of George Jones's country hymnal The Cup of Loneliness. The producers were – on purpose, I think – a little less subtle than usual: the ritual element of communion being used as a marketing tool seems fairly self-explanatory. But Don's baptism? Was it a nod to his own transformation from Dick to Don. Or the reverse? A spiritual resurrection and the end of "Don" as we know him?

NOTES

- Bert Cooper's marvellously catty sister is called Alice. Alice Cooper, presumably.

- Why was Betty bleeding? If it was menstrual blood surely it would be too much of a red herring to be remarked upon? Is she pregnant, as many of you speculated?

- Don was fixing a chair for Anna. Note his willingness to do this compared with his reluctance to fix things for Betty.

- The British firm is called Puttnam, Powell and Lowe. Likely a reference to British ad legends Chris Powell (BMP founder and the man behind the Smash aliens), Frank Lowe (Lowe & Partners) and David Puttnam who worked with Lowe at Collett Dickenson Pearce before working in film (along with colleagues Ridley Scott and Alan Parker).

- Pete: "How the hell did you swing that?" Peggy: "I'm sleeping with Don. It's really working out."

CULTURE WATCH

- The tune Anna is teaching when Don arrives is, her pupil explains, Grieg's In The Hall of the Mountain King from the Peer Gynt Suites, hence the episode's title. See Thoughts From The Typing Pool for more on the Gynt/Draper comparisons.

- The original The Day The Earth Stood Still from 1951 was on telly. In 2008 Jon Hamm starred in the remake.

THOUGHTS FROM THE TYPING POOL

AQuietMan Don fixing a chair for Anna, in contrast to him driving Betty into chair-smashing escapades was a metaphor so wide even I spotted it.

Digit The other thing about the rape is it besmirches the one area of Joan's life that really works – her perfect employee status. That's her main objection to having sex – the verboten location of Don's office – and that's why the guy forces her. It's a violation not just of her, but the relationships of trust she has around her.

SaintSnowy Joan's rape was one of the truly shocking moments in the show, yet you knew something like that was coming. There was an underlying unease about her doctor bloke anyway, particularly from a few episodes ago when he mentioned how she shouldn't be working, kept ordering her about to make his dinner and was dismissive of her work. His attack on her was even more depressing because it seemed to reflect not only his disgust at her prior sexual experience, but also her own resignation to his disgust. She almost looked like she was expecting it and that it was the price she had to pay for years of being sexually free. Maybe this shows that, despite what she might think of herself, she ultimately isn't quite as modern as she thinks she is.

IceniQueen It baffles me that a strong, intelligent woman like Joan would tolerate a man so obviously unstable just because he gives the illusion of stability. There doesn't even seem to be any sign of genuine love between them, they seem to be mutual status symbols. Surely Joan is savvy enough to realise her whole life will be one harrowing incident after another if she stays with Dr Jekyll. And for what, to show Roger Sterling that she has someone? To show Peggy that she may not have a career but she bagged the handsome doctor? I found the rape scene truly harrowing not only because Greg felt he had a right to punish Joan in this way but also because Joan didn't put up that much of a fight, it seemed like she would rather be robbed of her dignity rather than lose the status that being married to a doctor would bring her. Her look of resignation made me shudder.

DoraVale It's clear to us that Joan is being raped by her fiance, but is it clear to her? The idea of date rape gained credence only in the 1980s, and spousal rape was outlawed only relatively recently in many parts of America (and I wouldn't be surprised if there are still some states where it's still "legal").

This is before Women's Lib, and The Feminine Mystique has yet to be published. Women were not officially supposed to enjoy sex, and I suspect definitions of rape were much narrower back then – ie being forced to have sex with your husband, fiance etc would probably not have been defined as rape, even by the victim.

Insomniac506 Finally, we get to hear Don express what we've been thinking all season – that he sabotages his life, makes his family miserable, and that he's an observer of his own life, anaethetised and unhappy. I thought the scenes with Anna were acted beautifully, and their relationship was still eerily ambiguous – she seemed to be mother substitute, big sister, surrogate wife and shrink, with just a glimmer of sexual attraction. And what a delight to see Don introduce himself as "Dick" to the tight T-shirted boys and their big machines.

Betty seems to enjoy putting people to the test (in a very passive aggressive way, of course), arranging the chess pieces and basically organising the affair, so that when Sara Beth fails, she can judge her. I suspect it's a way for Betty to continue to demonstrate her own virtue. She can draw a line between "bad" Sara Beth and her own "good" self. Yes, it's petty, but let's face it, what else does Betty have to do?

DellaMirandola Betty really is the Rosamond Vincy [Bulstrode's niece in Middlemarch] of Mad Men: who wouldn't rather have mellow, lollipop-giving Anna (the living embodiment of Betty's Popsicle commercial) than uptight cupboard-locking hair-pulling Betty as wife and mother? And yet we also see Don telling Anna that he's fallen in love with Betty because she's such a happy laughing person. She didn't turn into Uptight Betty by herself – he and the world that surrounds her played a part in that.

JoeDoone Peggy's star is rising just as Pete's is waning. She has done a Don and made an excellent presentation, winning the Popsicles account, and she has done what none of the men dared, to ask for Freddy's office. Ken Cosgrove complains about their pre-pitch meeting taking place in a broom cupboard, but he does not join Harry Crane and Paul Kinsey in complaining that Peggy has won her own office.

Insomniac506 What a beautiful piece of writing as she absorbed Sal's mention of his mother breaking a Popsicle like a sacrament, channeling her own knowledge of Catholic ritual, and turning it into something almost as beautiful as Don's "Carousel" pitch for Kodak. Peggy's request to Roger for the office was delivered personally – Peggy is very emblematic of that first generation of women who made their own careers, walking a tightrope between being assertive and trying not to appear grabby and "unfeminine". How nice for her that Roger recognised she has more get up and go than her male colleagues.

RiverAngel There was a similarity between the "mother of the world" figure referred to by Anna in her Tarot card reading and the Virgin Mother. Their arms out posture is very similar albeit the Tarot figure is naked. Anna is, of course, a kind of mother to Dick/Don – giving him new life.

This feminine power/mother theme resonated throughout: Pete's refusal to let his wife be a mother, Dr Greg's refusal of Joan's own sexuality but imposition of his own, Betty's Mommy Dearest act with poor little Sally and haughty disapproval of her friend's sexuality.

Oldmuskrat Re: Peer Gynt …. How about Anna in the role of a "benevolent" troll princess (with awkward rolling gait) kind of a white witch/wise woman type? – the obverse to the conventionally beautiful but betrayed/bitter Betty/Solveig (Bets refers to her glum Nordic ancestry earlier in the series). Dick fits more with the womanising/wanderer Peer than Gatsby any day. He's the anti-Gatsby! He looks like he could toss away the American dream at any moment to live the simple blue-collar life.

EPISODE 13: Meditations In An Emergency

"To not thinking about things." THE MAN IN THE BAR

Betty is just about the centre of this episode. We open with her at the doctor's being given the news that she's been "blessed" with a child. She looked like she'd been told she was due to share a cell with Charles Bronson. With Don still estranged and her life in turmoil, it is, as she makes clear to the doctor, the last thing she needs.

The difficulty of abortion (another huge meta-theme for the writers to tackle), still illegal in New York for another eight years, led to a shot of Betty riding – consciously trying to give herself a miscarriage.

Anyway, her utter dread at the notion of a new baby and the apocalyptic atmosphere of the Cuban Missile Crisis set Betty off into the New York night with a Don-style mystery and swagger. Having dropped the kids off with Don in his hotel room, she lounges into a bar to be chatted up by a dark handsome stranger. Then it all went a bit Mills & Boon as, in her last stand before being once more enveloped by motherhood, she had no-strings anonymous sex with the chap in a private room in the back. In a lovely reversal of the norm, while Don was being Daddy and watching telly with the kids, she was nipping home in a post-coital fuzz to eat a chicken leg out of the fridge. Don would be, er, proud.

Was Betty's motivation a last stand of independence? Or was it more that, upon his return, Don had as good as confessed to his affair with Bobby (and tacitly his other affairs) giving Betty the excuse she needed to get her sexual vengeance?

Don seems liberated by his sojourn out west. Maybe Anna gave him one of those wind chimes. As well as apologising to Betty – once in person, once in a genuinely sweet letter – he seemed resigned to contentment at work. He finally gave Pete a bone and praised his work in California; he seemed fairly happy, too, to pick up his half million from the merger, and even happier to shove Duck's criticism down his throat and walk out on Sterling Cooper ("I don't have a contract" – boom).

Why bother working when he doesn't need to? The shot of him returning home to his (soon to be enlarged) family was as warm as any this series – and a lovely contrast to the last scene of season one, when Don returned defeated to an empty house. Maybe a new kid will do their battered marriage good?

Whether Don stays at SC or not remains to be seen. Duck certainly doesn't want him – but the PPL folks looked like they'd wondered what they'd done when Duck had his little rant in the boardroom. There was only ever going to be one winner in that particular battle of egos.

"This could be the end of the world and you could go to hell." FATHER GILL

Speaking of Peggy Olson, she – like Betty – was spurred on by the sense of doom to get the monkey (well, gorilla) off her back and finally reveal all to Pete about their illegitimate child. Here's a clue to the quality of the writing of this series (as if you need one): since Peggy had her baby, there's been one (one!) explicit mention of the fact – when Peggy's sister Anita confessed it to Father John. Everything else has been allusions, hints and visual nudges. And yet we're still hooked to know what happened.

Peggy finally admits the truth to Pete after he, drunkenly, told Peggy that he loved her and Peggy rebuffed his advances with the line, "I could have shamed you into being with me." Campbell looks like he's just been shot in the stomach as she tells him the truth about their child. *Still*, at least he's not firing blanks. Peggy leaves him alone in his office with only his antique gun for company.

For all the brilliance of the other characters, it's Pete who's the most fascinating. While the others are trying to find themselves, Pete knows who he is and, like (the similarly privileged) Betty, he's trying to escape from himself and his loveless marriage and his overbearing mother. What he wants, he has realised, is a lack of expectation. And Peggy Olson.

"He never could hold his liquor." SAINT JOHN POWELL

While all the emotional import was swirling between the Drapers and Peggy/Pete, the professional import is the impending takeover. As mentioned above, Duck was already showing signs that he might not have the temperament to run the company – or what's left of it, as he raged at Don's insouciance.

And what's not left of SC was what was worrying the four stooges – Sal, Kenneth, Harry and Paul – who used their charms to get the latest about the merger from the demoted Lois. After Harry – who's gone from bumbling to a bit nasty – patronised Lois to within an inch of her life ("Are they purchasing Sterling Cooper or are they *combining* it with them?" Lois: "It's a merger") they begin to fear for their careers.

So that was it. Once more everything is hanging by a thread and hardly anyone in the world of Sterling Cooper seems happy or content – except, paradoxically, the enigma that is Don Draper.

NOTES

- Don's payday from the merger is equivalent to $3.5m (£2.3m) today. Don had a 12% stake, which puts Sterling Cooper's value at about $42m (£28m).

- I hate the voiceover letter. But, like all those Mad Men touches, they get away with it – possibly because it was such an un-Don-like manoeuvre and admission of guilt. "Without you, I'll be alone for ever. I love you, Don."

- Pete with the gun. He definitely wasn't going to shoot himself, was he?

20TH CENTURY TALES

- We hear JFK making his 22 October speech announcing the beginning of the quarantine against Cuba.

THOUGHTS FROM THE TYPING POOL

LEA3012 The Pete/Peggy scene was absolutely brilliant. I was genuinely taken aback when Pete told Peggy he loved her and was surprised by the coldness with which Peggy delivered the news. She was almost smiling as the burden of guilt lifted off her shoulders, despite the fact that a man who had just professed his love sat crying in front of her. Just as Pete and Don finally get in touch with their sensitive sides, she is more detached than ever.

Digit Yeah, Duck totally blew it. He's out. These guys took one look at him losing his cool and thought, "not president material". Don, using the same verbal dexterity and confidence that's seen him triumph in every other sticky work situation thus far (and which Duck explicitly attempted to belittle) won even when he genuinely wasn't trying to. And Duck lost badly. He's made everyone else rich, but shot himself down in flames. The status quo maintained.

Insomniac506 I liked the way that Weiner and Co played on the normal expectations we have about Final Episodes and the catharsis that's supposed to follow big revelations. In this episode, we had the Big Speeches that we've been waiting for all season – Pete telling Peggy that he loves her, Peggy admitting that she had Pete's baby, Don telling Betty that he wants to be with her, Betty telling Don some (but not all) of the truth about her situation, Duck finally telling Don what he thinks about "those creative types". There was some release, but I think more for the audience than for the characters, who seemed as locked into their own miseries as before. This isn't the way TV is supposed to work – characters are supposed to discover truths about themselves, grow through the experience and become happier people.

Annick The final scene shows Don's reaction when he realises that Betty is only prepared to take him back because of her pregnancy. After his time away finding himself and his declaration of his love for Peggy in the letter, he is crushed to be told the reason she has asked him to come home. The series ends on a truly bittersweet note.

Bella79 The best moment of the whole episode for me was the boardroom meeting with PPL, Don's play of the no-contract card (lovely tip-off earlier when Duck made a joke about non-compete clauses), and Roger's almost mock-horror at it. He knew damn well that was what Don would do in response to Duck's radical plans – and I suspect that was always part of Roger and Cooper's plans. They knew Don wouldn't let Duck play the big man, and they also knew that the threat of the talented, and non-contracted, Don leaving would easily sway PPL into sidelining Duck. Masterful.

Insomniac506 I liked Betty's retort to Don when he comes to meet her at the riding club – how nice it is for men to be able to go off to take some time, and not worry about those left behind. It's the classic critique that the great heroes of our time have been men, because they have the freedom to wander, whereas the women are stuck back in the cave, tending the fire and looking after the spawn. Think Odysseus and Penelope – he goes to fight the Trojan War, she stays at home and embroiders. Thousands of years on, the sexual politics remain much the same.

Discussant It would be very un-Mad Men-like to close without some ambiguity. My interpretation of the ending is this: Don and Pete were on parallel courses, each maturing emotionally, revealing themselves more to the woman in their lives. The key is that they were both disappointed.

Pete, thinking the climax of his life has arrived and the woman he loves will admit her love for him, hears instead that she does not love him, and that she gave away their baby. All that growth on his part has led to a dead end. An inferior drama would have rewarded him somehow, but in Mad Men he gets nothing.

LucyT I don't think Joan was oblivious to Don and Betty's marriage problems [when she informs Don that Betty has asked him to come home]. She is a very intelligent secretary (and additionally she implies to Don that Bets has been calling the office a lot at one point). But unlike Jane, Joan would know that Don would find inappropriate levels of intimacy, sympathy or any trace of nudge-nudge signals unwelcome, that he would want their relationship to be warm yet professional.

It was sweet to see Don and Joan look at each other amusedly about Peggy's new hair and office. They are both fond of her in their own strange ways.

Bedelia [Re Betty developing a taste for dalliance] Yes, yes, yes. Remember when she tries to barter sex with the mechanic? She's rather disappointed that he turns her down. So obviously the fantasy is already there; and now she feels justified in playing it out. This might be the irony in series three – Don has come back from California with the memory of openness and rebirth with Anna Draper, and perhaps hopes that at some point he can tell the truth about Dick Whitman; but Betty is going the other way – she is now the one developing a secret life.

Meet the cast

**ELISABETH MOSS (PEGGY OLSON)
the woman behind the secretary
turned star copywriter...**

PHIL HOGAN

It's close to cocktail hour when Elisabeth Moss comes blowing in on a freezing blast of New York, a tiny figure wrapped up in one of those big, quilted coats that looks like a sleeping bag with arms. "Coldest day of the year," she says, cheerfully as we head up in the lift to the hotel's "reading" room, with its fluting lounge music and view of the twinkling lights on Madison Avenue.

She apologises for being late, the result of having just moved in with her boyfriend (comedian Fred Armisen, a cast member of Saturday Night Live) uptown, which was confusing for her publicist, who arranged for a car to be sent to her old place downtown and had to divert it, which was then confusing for the driver. But doesn't she have to be on stage at eight? Oh, there's plenty of time, she says, rightly sensing that I'm more worried about my interview time ticking away than keeping her audience waiting.

Moss is best known for her portrayal of Peggy, the ingenuous young secretary in Mad Men, and when we meet is playing another ingenuous young secretary, Karen, in a revival of David Mamet's Speed-the-Plow, a satire of 80s Hollywood chicanery.

It seems a superficial similarity but aren't both women trying to make themselves heard in the great male conversation? Yes, says Moss, though in different ways. "Peggy is prim and quiet, whereas Karen is outspoken, brutally truthful, says what she feels – can't help but tell the truth."

Moss hasn't done theatre since she first moved to New York as a 19-year-old, and this – a three-hander, with longtime Mamet collaborator William H Macy and Raúl Esparza ("He's a genius") playing a pair of bottom-feeding movie executives – is her Broadway debut. "It's fantastic," she says, but also "an emotional, physical and mental marathon. Eight shows a week is very difficult. I did Mad Men for four months until the end of August, then started rehearsals here in early September. But I get to work with the most amazing actors – and do Mamet, which is unusual for a woman. There aren't that many female parts, so I feel lucky that I got one."

Moss was raised in Los Angeles, in what she calls an "artistic household". Her father is British and manages jazz musicians and her mother is from Chicago and plays blues harmonica (with the likes of BB King). Her younger brother is in the movie business, but "on the other side of the camera". She went to a small private school which was "very focused, very academic – but there was no extra-curriculum". She graduated early at 15.

Then what – college? Stage training? "No, I just kept working, kept acting. I was a dancer for years. I've done everything. Big parts in indie films, small parts in big films, TV movies, one or two commercials. I've been acting for 20 years."

She's 26 now. At 15, she was the burns victim in Girl, Interrupted, a film set in a mental institution in the 60s and starring Winona Ryder and Angelina Jolie. Then at 17 she got what turned out to be her big break, in The West Wing, as Zoey Bartlet, the president's daughter. She was on the show for seven years. Was her political outlook formed during those years? "Well, it's a very liberal show, but it was more that – it was a very smart show. I was probably formed more by the intelligence of it than the politics. The writing was so smart and spot-on. When you have writing like that, you almost don't have to do anything, so I felt I was influenced more creatively."

I ask if she is looking forward to the Obama presidency. "I was in New York when he won and I've never seen the city like that. It felt almost like an episode of The West Wing – this idealism you could see in everyone. The excitement and positivity was incredible."

Did the frenetic pace of The West Wing help when it came to doing Mamet? "Absolutely. Mamet is a very different writer, of course, but the intelligence and pace are very similar."

It's some contrast to Mad Men, I say, with its unhurried storylines and dawdling shots of people having a long think. "The pace and the style of it was so completely different from anything I'd ever done. It's teasing, as opposed to being explicit like Mamet or Sorkin [creator of The West Wing]. But I think all of us [in the show] agree that we were attracted by that pilot script. The show was on a network that no one really knew. People knew who Matthew Weiner was because of The Sopranos [on which he was a writer and producer], but he'd never created his own show. There were no stars, and advertising in the 60s didn't sound like a winner – but the writing was so good."

I wonder if she felt a cultural shift with Mad Men – moving from a huge show to one that was only shown on cable? "You'd think there would have been, except that cable is big right now. There's been this incredible resurgence of cable programming – shows like Dexter and Damages, and HBO, obviously. Many years ago, there would have been a difference but now it's about the same. Plus, for me, it's a different thing anyway – The West Wing was a recurring thing, whereas Mad Men is regular."

She auditioned twice for the part of Peggy. "It just felt like a really good fit. I remember calling my manager after meeting

Matt [Weiner] and saying I could work with that man. There was an immediate connection artistically. I think I did the part he wrote, and he saw that, and I knew it."

Mad Men oozes class, with critics and fans falling over themselves to praise its visual sophistication (the opening credit sequence of a silhouetted man slowly falling through the canyons of Manhattan is worth the entrance fee alone) and authentic handling of time and place. The LA Times said Mad Men had found "a strange and lovely space between nostalgia and political correctness and filled it with interesting people, all of them armed with great power of seduction". Entertainment Weekly identifies an America "free of self-doubt, guilt and counter-cultural confusion. It's the ripe fantasy before it turns rotten."

But it's the way the characters keep you guessing that keeps you watching. You assume from the start that the agency's creative chief, Don Draper (Jon Hamm), is the complicated one, but then you see the parallels emerging with Peggy, the frumpish new girl from out in the sticks whose talents start to shine. Moss is compelling as Peggy. She's the one who sees a horizon beyond this modern "clever" Manhattan set, whose lives – artificially illuminated by liquor and leisure and consumer fads – contain an inherent struggle for contentment of the sort seen in the vogueish, rediscovered fiction of Richard Yates (Revolutionary Road) and Sloan Wilson, whose novel The Man in the Gray Flannel Suit is knowingly referenced in the new series. Nervy but watchful, Peggy sits amid the vulgarity of office life like a Buddha. You can almost hear her brains ticking. You just have to root for her. Was her development clear from the outset?

"Even I was guilty of thinking that maybe it was going to be a storyline where she claws her way to the top and sleeps with Don, but it doesn't go that way at all. What ends up happening is so much richer and so much more interesting. The thing about Don and Peggy that is obviously similar is they both have a secret they can't talk about. They're both very private people. They both just want to do their jobs."

To an extent, the depths of Don's existential angst have been fathomed for us (the hidden shame in his past that makes a daily misery of his handsomeness and his nice suits and successful career and beautiful wife), but Peggy seems harder to read – innocent but ambitious, self-contained but with unpredictable bursts of cruelty. She always seems capable of surprise. "It really is a great part. As an actor, you're always trying to play subtext or not say what you mean. So being given a character that does only that is really interesting."

Looking at practically everyone in the show – the super-groomed Draper, the reptilian junior exec Pete, the rest of the goofy ad team, the pneumatically stacked office man-eater Joan – it's tempting to marvel at the care that went into the casting, but seeing Moss here now (dark, slim, stylish, attractive; frankly, not really any of the things that Peggy is), that assumption starts to look a bit misguided. Of course, her character's dumpy looks and terrible hair and unworldly dress sense weren't helped by her getting fatter and fatter (or, as it turned out, pregnant – unknown to everyone, including herself) during the first series. "We went through this very meticulous process of making Peggy realistically gain weight. I had, like, four stages of padding and then two stages of prosthetic make-up. Thankfully, I wasn't asked to do it myself, which I would have done, but it would have been harder."

To put weight on?

She laughs. "To take it off again."

Did she mind playing the least glamorous girl in Manhattan?

"I enjoyed the second season more because we got to make everything a bit smaller and tighter and shorter. Not drastically – Peggy is still Peggy, but she definitely gets to wear nicer things."

Given that Moss wasn't born until 1982, I wonder how well she knew the era – this pre-revolutionary, pre-women's lib 60s. Was she shocked by how benighted and unswinging it was?

"I think so. I had a surface understanding. But this was on the tail-end of the 50s. You really are on the cusp of change – this carry-over from that earlier mentality. There's a little bit of the beatnik thing that's touched upon. The second season is different."

It is. A huge Xerox machine arrives in the office. A new accent on youth is signalled with the appearance of young creatives sporting cable knits rather than suits. Peggy represents this coming of the proper 60s too, of course, settling into her new post as junior copywriter, armoured by foreknowledge, it almost seems, against the spite of her male colleagues, laughing their foolish heads off. They are the ones whom history will sweep aside.

With its heavy freight of period misogyny, it's hard not to take against the alpha males, even though, as Moss says, Weiner is simply telling it how it was. "It doesn't really take men or women's sides."

Perhaps not, but the eye of the writer is a modern one and the temptation to even up the battle with some strong women's roles was clearly important. Is there anything of herself in Peggy? "With all of the characters in that show, each of the actors brings a huge part of themselves to it. That's the fun of it, figuring out which parts of yourself you can bring and which are different. Peggy and I have a lot of similarities. She's also a very positive person. She believes in the good of people. She's not conniving. She tries to do the right thing."

Career-wise, it's not bad going, I say, to follow up The West Wing with another huge hit. What's it like to be an overnight sensation after 20 years? "Well, things have changed. And I do actually get recognised a lot. It always surprises me. I'll stand outside in the street and people will be, 'Peggy! Peggy!' But it's been a slow burn. I like that people really love the show and associate me with it. I don't seek it out – being a celebrity – but if it happens I'm glad it's for something that I'm proud of."

Does she have other ambitions – a big movie maybe?

"To me, the writing is important. It's helped me get into some really good shows. I wouldn't change that."

But what if someone came along and wanted to give you millions to play Wonder Woman?

"Well, I wouldn't say I wouldn't do a huge movie if it was a great script. You have to do things for the right reasons. The material is the important thing." Anyway, she points out, things have changed. It's not as if TV actors still seek validation from doing movies. "You look at American TV now and you've got Glenn Close, Holly Hunter, Sally Field – incredible female actors who have won Oscars and they're doing television shows. Film used to be more 'respected'; now it's not like that."

She prefers, too, the camaraderie of TV – and latterly theatre – where intense work and close proximity for long seasons make for lasting friendships. She has also developed a taste for awards ceremonies. Mad Men has won a shelf of prizes including six Emmys and three Golden Globes (two for the show, one for Jon Hamm); Moss is nominated this year for a Screen Actors Guild award for outstanding female actor. "I've been fortunate in that the last few awards parties we've been to we've won. I hear it's not so much fun when you don't. It's a great chance to hang out together and catch up."

Does she drink? In fact, does she smoke

No!

So who in the cast smokes? She won't say. I only ask, of course, because Mad Men is notorious for its 60-an-episode habit. She laughs. "Isn't that funny? Everyone who saw it was like, 'They're

SMOKING! They're SMOKING!' No one noticed they were cheating on their wives."

Theatre calls. I wish her luck. I'm not sure if American thespians say "break a leg". In this weather, it seems to be asking for trouble.

1963

Season Three

EPISODE ONE: Out Of Town

"You're an ambitious man, and an ambitious man is never happy with what he has." TRUDY CAMPBELL

We're six months on from where we left off at the end of series two. It's April 1963, the Cuban missile crisis hasn't killed everyone thankfully, and despite the turmoil at the end of 1962 (ie Pete telling Peggy he loved her) not a lot seems to have happened to the major characters. Although Betty is bags-packed close to giving birth.

The main unrest seems to have come with the arrival of the Brits via the Duck-engineered merger with PPL. One-third of the Sterling Cooper staff have been let go and Duck is long gone too. The final sacking, that of previously unseen head of accounts Burt Peterson (who must have replaced Duck), welcomes us back into this new world. The company though, is much expanded and a spot of, as Roger puts it, "playing God, or playing Darwin" by new CFO Lane Pryce (played by Jared Harris) has left Ken and Pete as the joint heads of accounts.

When Pete finds out that he isn't where the buck stops his reaction is typically one of apoplexy and genuine confusion. It's not necessarily entitlement, more that he's cast himself as a martyr despite his success. "Why can't I get anything good all at once?" he begs of Trudy. Ken, typically, takes it in his stride like an Ivy League essay writing contest. Pete doesn't ask about wages because he mainly craves status and he often seems intimidated by the bosses. Ken has no such qualms. As Cosgrove points out: it's going to be an interesting battle.

Don, meanwhile, is "celebrating" Dick's Birthday and has gone past flashbacks, and is now imagining/recreating his own birth as he boils some milk. The imminent arrival of his third child draws up hazy notions of his stepmother miscarrying, while his own mother died in childbirth. The main, rather morbid, thing we learn is that he was named Dick because his mother's last wish was to cut off Don's father's dick for doing this to her. Having Don break a thick skin on the milk as he recollects/imagines the story of his birth is a clever directorial touch. The (excellent) TV blogger Alan Sepinwall makes the point that the story of his being unwanted has probably been drummed into Don's head by his stepmother all his young life. Therefore he's especially keen to reassure Sally (and Betty for that matter) that she's loved and wanted. After she told him that she broke his suitcase he tells her: "I'll always come home, you'll always be my girl."

"Limit your exposure." LONDON FOG CAMPAIGN SLOGAN

The major point of narrative is Sal and Don's trip to the London Fog Coat Company in Baltimore. After utilising an old suitcase label to trick two buxom air hostesses who look like Thunderbirds into thinking that they are spooks looking into dodgy Teamster leader James Hoffa, Don (who revels in spinning the yarn) inevitably, and unashamedly, takes one of the girls back to his room. Sal, meanwhile, makes subtle eyes at a bellboy in the lift. A quick broken air conditioning switch later and he finds himself nervously in flagrante – so it is with a mixture of relief and regret that they are interrupted by a fire alarm before anything major can happen. But it's enough for Don – as he climbs down the fire escape – to get the picture. He's not a man to blab other people's secrets – and the gentle nudge he gives Sal via the "limit your exposure" campaign for London Fog spells out the fact that while he is happy to ignore it, he ought to watch what he is doing.

NOTES

- Betty critiques Sally: "She's taken to your tools like a little lesbian."

- The list of accounts that are divvied out between Ken and Pete show just how much the merger has bulked out SC's standing.
  The list in full is: Bacardi, Belle Jolie, Birds Eye, Cadbury, Campbell's Soup International, Cartwright Double Sided Aluminium, Chevron Oil, Dunkin' Donuts, General Foods Europe, Kodak, Lever Brothers, Martinson's, Popsicle, Relaxerciser, Rio de Janeiro (which is dormant), United Fruit, Warner Brothers (Ken's portfolio) and Admiral Television, Alpine Real Estate, Bethlehem Steel, Consolidated Edison, Gilette, Gorton's, Liberty Capital Savings, Lucky Strike, Maytag, North American Aviation, Proctor and Gamble, Pampers, Playtex, Samsonite, Seacore Laxatives, Schneider's Ketchup, Utz (Pete's portfolio).

- Great last words from Burt Peterson: "Fellow comrades in mediocrity, I want you to listen very carefully … you can all go straight to hell."

- Peggy refers to John Hooker (Pryce's right hand man) as "Moneypenny". Miaow. Meanwhile, fans of late 90s ITV comedy dramas might recognise actor Ryan Cartwright from The Grimleys.

- Don on his brother-in-law (and himself) – "He never tires of putting his name on other people's things."

CULTURE WATCH

- Bert Cooper's Rothko has taken second place to The Dream Of The Fisherman's Wife by Great Wave painter Hokusai. Another nod to Cooper's Japanophilia. Although what the picture, an octopus performing cunnilingus, means is open to debate. "I picked it for its sensuality," offers Bert.

- The dynamic between the father and son of London Fog is reminiscent of the relationship between Swede Levov and his father at the Newark Maid glove company in Philip Roth's American Pastoral.

- Air hostess Shelly compares Don to actor Tyrone Power. Who died at just 44 of a heart attack. An omen?

- "Our worst fears lie in anticipation" Sal tellingly channels Balzac during the London Fog meeting. The actual quote should be: "Our worst misfortunes never happen, and most miseries lie in anticipation."

THOUGHTS FROM THE TYPING POOL

Bella79 I genuinely don't think that there will be a better shot on TV all year than Don's face at Sal's window. I love Hamm's face when Draper is shocked; he always goes a little bit Dick Whitman for a moment.

Digit Maybe it's because I just finished RD Laing's The Divided Self, but Don's compulsive philandering suddenly made more sense to me than it ever had before. The split his own sense of unwantedness as a child has created in him is a powerful need to make his own family feel wanted, but also a need to perpetually reassure himself of his own desirability through promiscuity – the second need coming, unsurprisingly, into conflict with the first.

Oldmuskrat He does seem to have a split personality when it comes to relationships with women. The air stewardess liaison seems like a new low really (almost like Betty's unknown man in bar encounter). Sally finding the mislaid stewardess pin brooch in his case was brilliant, he did look a bit queasy for about a nano-second.

DellaMirandola Can Don really keep his promise to Sally [to always come home] if he's going to spend his time shagging random stewardesses? And is it better or worse for him to be now engaging in fairly meaningless casual sex as opposed to the more serious mistresses we've seen in previous series?

I didn't like the British very much – too stereotypical. Did the British gurus like Ogilvy who led the world in the 1960s really get to the top by being traditional British stuffed shirts? For a drama like Mad Men which loves surprising us with characters' complexity and evocation of the period, it's a bit of a disappointment to find that they can't give us the kind of Brit who fell in love with the energy of America in the 1950s/60s and wanted to move away from traditional British boring ideas and capture some of that energy for themselves.

Digit Bear in mind that these Brits aren't volitional expats like Ogilvy; they've been posted to NYC. Still, that only really excuses the Lane character and I agree that Hooker is a bit ridiculous.

EPISODE TWO: Love Among The Ruins

Peggy, as Roger acknowledges in the lift, flies a different route from the other girls. While the men drool over Ann-Margret making puppy eyes at the screen, she's rightly more concerned that, as a sell, it's appealing to men rather than women. What *is* surprising is Don's agreeing with the boys – he's normally the first to spot these things. The subtext that she is never going to be that kind of girl is clear, which makes the moment when Peggy sings in front of the mirror all the more surprising.

The subway references are a clever way of dealing with this. In episode one, Joan mentioned that she'd never ride on the subway while Peggy, as our independent woman, was happy to do so – despite it not being so safe. We then heard Joan's "I feel like I'm on the subway line" which Peggy – emerging from the tube out to a Brooklyn bar – uses to start a conversation with the engineering student. This goes back to the idea of the women being two sides of the same coin; a thread that's developed since series one.

The fact that Peggy is bold enough to go into the bar and make idle chit-chat seems more important than the fact that she had sexual relations with the guy. You wonder if her confidence is either a reaction to the goo-goo sensuality of Ann-Margret or a step away from it?

"The plans, the plans, the plans you make." GENE HOFSTADT

Meanwhile, up in Ossining, the debate over Gene continues. Betty seems motivated more by jealousy of her sister-in-law's nursing and William's inheritance than a genuine desire to help her father. Perhaps that's unfair, but Don's intervention – and complete emasculation of William – solves matters. Is his decision to move Gene in with them motivated mainly by a desire to stop Betty worrying/complaining? The addition of a new person in their home ought to add an interesting new dynamic to an already terse household. Gene hearing sirens, thinking it was the 1920s, and draining away Don's booze may be an omen of what's to come. We leave the Drapers at Sally's maypole ceremony, with Don hiding his gaze at Sally's beautiful teacher behind his aviators. Is she to be a new paramour – or does she remind him of someone else?

"You have no problems with an atom plant on the East River, but this bothers you?" PETE

The main bit of office action – aside from Patio – is Pete's pitch for the redevelopment of Penn Station into Madison Square Garden. Kinsey – whose ethics seem as consistent as a beardy liberal's on Madison Avenue can be – nearly blew the whole deal by agreeing with the protesters. The weaving of not particularly obvious non-fictional 60s moments, but important ones nevertheless (like the plane crash last year), is one of my favourite aspects of the show. And the way Weiner uses it here as a way to highlight SC's move into the murkier world of

Bernays-style PR as well as normal advertising is a terrific trick. One that could be done badly so easily.

NOTES

- Roger's daughter's wedding is on November 23, 1963. The day after John F Kennedy gets shot in Dallas.

- Don's son Bobby is a new actor (Jared Gilmore), the second time he's changed. He changed after series one too.

- "I work for a jerk." No one hears Peggy's comment in the bar – she's referring to Don, right?

- Don, we learn, didn't bring anyone to his wedding. How on earth did he get away with that? Not to mention getting their anniversary wrong.

20TH CENTURY TALES

- Pryce's wife snidely says – "We're near the UN, so there's plenty of Africans" in reference to the process of decolonization centred at the time around the United Nations.

- The journalist referred to by the MSG execs was the New York Times' fabled architecture critic Ada Louise Huxtable.

- Roger refers to Paul making a "Yetta Wallenda-sized misstep" in reference to the acrobat who fainted at the top of the top of a fibreglass pole, fell 50ft and died in Omaha, Nebraska.

CULTURE WATCH

- The most obvious reference was Cosgrove's Patio team watching Ann-Margret sing the theme from the movie version of the 1960 musical Bye, Bye Birdie (released April 4 1963).

- The song in the bar is To Be Loved by The Pentagons.

- The episode is called Love Among The Ruins – a nod to the poem of the same name by Robert Browning?

THOUGHTS FROM THE TYPING POOL

Dominia My take on Don and Gene is that Don is simply displaying his Mr Fix-It skills that he brings to any crisis or stalemate in the office, usually with great success. His payoff is playing alpha male over William, possibly also taking the heat off his marriage a little, but the price could be quite high – losing his whisky being just the beginning.

Digit Peggy's bar pickup seemed to be mainly about the dawning of women's liberation and, *pari passu*, a new confidence in her. It's a bit like Sex & The City where one of the characters has sex "like a man". Peggy's older than her conquest, she lies to him, she takes a bite of his burger without asking, she has things to teach him and hence, crucially, isn't ashamed of revealing she's experienced. At the end, when he tentatively suggests they might do it again, she's clearly not bothered and departs with a dismissive, "this was fun". It's as if, when she plays Ann-Margret in front of the mirror, she's trying it on just to confirm for herself how bullshit it is. Is this what men want? Screw that, she thinks, I'm going to play it my way; and she immediately goes out and does.

Bell79 I couldn't decide whether Don simply fancied the teacher, or whether he saw something in there for the Patio campaign, and decides that Peggy might be right. But the hand under the chair, harking back to his words to Betty at the start of the first episode ("you're on a warm sandy beach … ") strikes me as the escapist Don that we saw in California, secretly revelling in the freedom of the dance and the grass.

DrQuinzel The shot of Don touching the grass – how gorgeous. He apparently revels in his life selling lies from 50-feet above the city, but he just wants to get down to earth once in a while, to connect with something natural. But it's the fact that he hides this like it's a guilty secret, touching the grass like an embarrassed teenage masturbator, that makes this moment so brilliant. All part of his wonderful dual nature.

DellaMirandola Bye Bye Birdie was *huge* in 1963 – and it was supposed to encapsulate what being a "young person" was all about. I agree that the juxtaposition between that articifial "youthful vigour" and the proto-hippy simplicity at the end was a key theme in the episode. Peggy trying on the Ann-Margret mode for size is just doing what young women across the country were doing at the time. It's a nice illustration of how things have moved on since the Jackie versus Marilyn debate. Then, the options were to be a sophisticate like Jackie or a sensual woman like Marilyn. Now it's being a teen but a teen in heavy heavy makeup, with superglued hair, singing manufactured pop. Or the choice which isn't really available to Peggy yet – of being a boho flower child naturally singing folk music.

EPISODE THREE: My Old Kentucky Home

"I'm Peggy Olson. And I want to smoke some marijuana."
PEGGY

With Peggy, Smitty and Kinsey stuck in the office, the scene is set for Peggy to take another step away from the girl we met in series one. After last week's action in the bar, she's happy to join the boys in a green haze as they struggle to come up with ideas for Bacardi – the weed fuzz eventually provides some inspiration to Peggy, and also leaves another layer of her unravelled. Most important, however, are her scenes with the new secretary, Olive, who represents the conformity that Peggy is beginning to rail against. Her state-of-a-generation speech to Olive sums this up perfectly: "I have a secretary, that's you. And I'm not scared of any of this. But you're scared. Don't worry about me, I'm going to do everything you want for me."

"People don't think you're happy. They think you're foolish." DON

Roger's garden party provided the perfect opportunity to expand on the animosity between Don and Roger that has already been hinted at. So we see Roger, in blackface, serenading Jane in front of a laughing crowd, with Don and Pete apparently the only ones not amused. It's difficult to assess mid-1960s attitudes with the benefit of 21st century hindsight (something the show is keen to reinforce) but given that by 1964, Mummer's parades in nearby Philadelphia had banned people from donning blackface, one imagines that by this point it must have been known that it was offensive. On the other hand, the Black and White Minstrel Show ran in the UK until 1978 – so, in context, perhaps it's not that shocking.

Either way, Don can't watch. He meets a similar soul, Connie (who we later learn is hotel magnate Conrad Hilton), at the bar, and tells him more in three minutes than 95% of the people he's met in the show. Regarding Roger, I'd guess that Don's resentment of him and Jane comes from their affair leading to the sale of the firm, which threatened Don's cosy position. Or is he just annoyed that Roger had the temerity to actually end his unhappy marriage? No doubt the friction will run and run. We left the party with Don and Betty in as touching as an embrace as they've had for a long time. But Betty's chat with the man from the governor's office hints that there's still more angst to come.

"You people think money is the solution to everything." GENE

Sally stealing Gene's $5 was intriguing. The shots of them reading together established a closeness. But what – for Sally – was a bit of juvenile thieving, inadvertently highlights her grandfather's helplessness with his situation. Both Betty and Carla assume that the money has been misplaced rather than stolen, but Sally's butter-wouldn't-melt "Grandpa! Is this it?"

doesn't fool Gene. Touchingly, rather than shout at her (as she expected) he invites her back to read his book to him.

Joan, meanwhile, after a wonderfully passive aggressive and subtext-laden chat with Jane in the office ("I just stopped by to have my rings resized"), was hosting some of Greg's colleagues and their wives for dinner. Their relationship seems fairly normal after the incident in season two, but there's still hurt in Joan's eyes, and she acquiesces to Greg's table-setting demands – although she still manages a wonderful recital of C'est Magnifique on the accordion. The chat with Jane, though – with the new Mrs Stirling's driver circling outside – only reaffirms what Joan's parallel life could have been like.

NOTES

- Sterling Cooper's boho intellectual Paul Kinsey is actually a Jersey boy who got into Princeton on a scholarship. I love the glimpse of backstory of him being kicked out of the (still-going) Tiger Tones acapella male singing group.

- During Pete and Trudy's well-practised dance at the party, Pete constantly looks up towards Don and Bert to see if they were watching him and approving.

20TH CENTURY TALES

- Roger refers to the wedding of divorcee Happy Murphy to New York governor (and future vice-president) Nelson Rockefeller. Roger says "Now we'll be stuck with Goldwater." Meaning that the scandal would ruin the governor's run at the presidency. Which it did.

CULTURE WATCH

- Sally was reading Edward Gibbon's 1776 classic, The History of the Decline and Fall of the Roman Empire, to Gene.

- The song that Roger sings (and gives this episode its title) is the pre-sanitised version of Kentucky's state song My Old Kentucky Home.

- Kinsey and Geoffrey's touching sing-song was to Howard and Emerson's Hello! Ma Baby! which – interestingly, given Roger's performance – originated as a minstrel show-inspired "coon song".

- "This is the way the world ends …" Kinsey shows off his literary smarts by reciting the last verse of TS Eliot's The Hollow Men. A favourite of Apocalypse Now's Colonel Kurtz, no less.

- Connie refers to the 1935 film version of "Midsummer Dream" with Mickey Rooney.

TECHNICAL NOTE

Listen out in future episodes for the delicious use of sound bridges by the directors. There are three great ones here: Peggy getting high over the banjo notes of Roger's song; Kinsey reciting Eliot over Pete and Trudy's dance; and Sally reading about the fall of the Romans over the final shot of the marquee.

THOUGHTS FROM THE TYPING POOL

SuperSpartan Interesting to see Pete displaying liberal attitudes that we might not have expected from him, given his background. I remember something similar when Kurt came out and most of the men in the office were sniggering about it. Pete, returning from California with oranges, didn't seem perturbed by, or disapproving of that, in contrast to people like Crane, and Cosgrove. Perhaps that, and the dancing with Trudy, shows that he's the genuinely youthful one amongst them.

JoeDoone Sally's reading of Gibbon went nicely with the revelries at the party and the marijuana on Madison Avenue, and with the coming fall of Camelot.

Bella79 The very wonderful Alan Sepinwall's blog points out that Roger, Pete and Betty are all having a fine time at the party because this is the privileged world in which they grew up; Don and Jane, however, are struggling because this is new to them.

Dominia Who says the USA has no class structure? The contrasts of class, age and style between the three social events at the end were superb, as well as each being perfect in itself. Roger's party is square but has all the high-class glamour, while the dope scene looks almost squalid in contrast. But Peggy is the winner, the only one to come out of the event with ideas and inspiration which you know she'll use creatively. Did anyone else find Joan's dinner party unutterably sad? She now discovers she's married down, to an incompetent jerk, who humiliates her by making her perform a silly dated song in a ridiculous French accent.

Digit The humour of that line [Peggy's "I'm so high"] and the slack-jawed applause, is in the way that it's code for, "I am totally detached from what I've just experienced." The scene seems to me to perfectly express the once subversive effect of marijuana (probably because dope smoking is so common now). Suddenly the old cliché about dope being a way of liberating the mind from the shackles of convention seems to have some validity. So much of Mad Men is about us seeing the normality of the era as something almost hallucinatorily bizarre.

Insomniac506 The distinction between the landed ruling classes and the up-and-comers has never seemed more profound. Peggy and the worker mice left in the office for the weekend while the WASPs trip off to the country club, and then a subtle class differentiation between fat, geeky slightly-too-desperate Harry Crane and his wife not being allowed to sit with the cool kids.

Don seems to be the only one capable of some kind of dissent, even though his trance-like expression suggests he was quite happy to "pass" and keep the peace. When Don gets around rich people, he gets deeply uncomfortable and pale – it's delicious to watch – and his facial expressions hover somewhere between "I've made it" and a silent self-reminder to blend in.

JoeDoone To those naysayers who say that Mad Men moves with the speed of a constipated glacier, remember Gene's wise words to Sally when her reading of Gibbon is suspended by her bedtime: "You just wait. All hell's going to break loose."

EPISODE FOUR: The Arrangements

"You don't want to hear about it, Scarlett O'Hara." GENE

The glorious opening scene with Sally chauffeuring Gene sets up an exploration of Gene, Betty and Sally's relationship. This episode is called The Arrangements – referring to Gene's funeral plans. Despite an ill Gene taking care of everything, Betty's response is to, in effect, cover her ears and tell him he's "selfish and morbid". Gene's assessment of her wanting to be shielded from dangers ("That's why you married that joker") is accurate – and she proves it with her reaction to his funeral planning.

Things are simpler with his granddaughter. Gene is the first person to talk to Sally lovingly and affirmatively and, between telling her that's she's smart, he lets slip that her mother was chubby as a kid, which goes someway to explaining Betty's snippiness towards her daughter's looks. These scenes with Gene and Sally are some of the warmest Mad Men have ever offered us. And – after we find out about Gene's death – what a wonderful performance from young Kiernan Shipka, as she's literally locked out of her mother's grieving by the front door and later screams at her parents for morbidly laughing. Betty's reaction to Sally ("You're being hysterical") may have been heartless, but we know she's grieving too. Sadly, the only way she can express it is by eating one of her father's peaches.

"Jack Kennedy certainly ended up with a better job than his father." DON

In the office, one of Pete's old Dartmouth chums, Horace ("Ho Ho") – another Fitzgeraldy-type – is trying to prove himself to his dad by pumping his inheritance into a national Jai Alai league. His naivety and $3m ad budget send Sterling Cooper's finest into a froth. Don's objections to the milking of the fatted calf lead to the scene where Ho Ho's father is brought into Cooper's office to check whether they should proceed. Horace's father has no faith in Jai Alai ("Are you drunk? It's like Polish handball") and even less in his son ("My son lives in a cloud of success, but it's my success"). It's fair enough, but Horace can't win here – he succeeds and it's down to his father, fails and it's his own fault.

Likewise, a few of Sterling Cooper's males live, like Ho Ho, in the shadow of their fathers (Pete and Roger for a start). Don is the opposite, having outgrown his disastrous upbringing. His inheritance extends to his face and one black and white photo of his parents.

NOTES

- Peggy is also having trouble with a parent. Her transparent attempt to distract her mum with an Admiral TV show that the aftershocks of her pregnancy still reverberate in the Olson household.

- I loved the mismatch between new housemates Karen and Peggy – prom queen meets wallflower – despite Peggy's job and office. Elisabeth Moss did a great job of conveying Peggy's nervousness – "I like ... fun."

- Joan's immediate redrafting of Peggy's "flatmate wanted" ad once more showed that she's a copywriting natural.

- After his flamboyant run through of the Patio ad, it looks like Kitty has twigged about Sal's sexuality.

- Roger calls it right on the Patio ad: "She's not Ann-Margret." You can try and appropriate culture for business, but you have to be either subtle or go all out (ie, hire the actress and do it properly).

20TH CENTURY TALES

- Peggy's mum is waiting to hear more news on the death of Pope John XXIII (d. 3 June).

- When Peggy's mother turns on the news we hear JFK discussing Vivian Malone and James Hood's attempts to enter the University of Alabama. Later the report mentions Thích Quang Đú'c setting himself on fire in Vietnam. Oddly, these two defining images of the decade happened on the very same day – 11 June.

CULTURE WATCH

- As far as I can tell, the director who quit the Patio ad to go to LA – "George Cohan/Cohen" was fictional. But the song used over the final credits – WWI song and nod to Gene – Over There was written by George M Cohan, a great subtle touch. That, like Bye Bye Birdie, has recently been appropriated by an ad agency in the UK, for a series of awful ads for insurance comparison site Go Compare.

- Joan nods to one of MM's key references when she observes Peggy's ad is "like the stage directions from an Ibsen play".

- Horace was reading original Mad Man David Ogilvy's Confessions Of An Advertising Man.

THOUGHTS FROM THE TYPING POOL

JoeDoone The absence of Ann-Margret aside, surely the reason why the ad, so ably directed by Sal, fails is because it is for a drink called Patio. Who would want to drink a drink called Patio? It should be buried under Beth Jordache's dad.

SuperSpartan What a look on Pete's face when Don tried to talk Horace out of the idea over dinner. You'd have thought that when Horace saw that he'd have realised that Don was telling the truth. Perhaps that's why Don subsequently lost sympathy for him (hence "bill it to the kid" when he breaks the ant farm).

Bella79 Gene's death and Sally's outburst actually made me cry, which is the first time MM has done that. God, Betty's a horrible mother, isn't she? And I was even disappointed with Don who, for all we know he loves his children, didn't exactly redeem himself (I was shouting "will someone just hug her!" at the screen the whole time). Along with Gene calling her "Scarlett O'Hara", this whole episode in itself was harking back quite beautifully to something else within Gone With the Wind, when it's pointed out to Scarlett that children and parents never see eye to eye or often like each other, but that grandparents and grandkids generally admire each other – which we can definitely see in Sally and Gene.

Insomniac506 Sally's learning, poor little mite, that the early 1960s is not a world where parents care about their children, particularly when mommy is a daddy's girl who's still a child herself. Gene gave as much psychological clarity to Betty's personality in a few small scenes as anyone's managed to so far – she's a spoiled over-indulged princess, who was driven to thinness by an overly obsessive mother and shielded from life by a doting father. Fast-forward to the Summer of Love and I guarantee Sally will be smoking pot and dancing topless in the mud with the other hippies at Woodstock. Either that or she'll be in therapy and miserable. In the meantime, she has to sit under the table in her ballet tutu crying

HerrDobler To the uninitiated, the scene with Peggy and her mother would have been a comical scene about a mother who can't let go – but we know exactly why Peggy's mother is so afraid for her daughter. And in the context of the Pope just having died, this is a sad day for Peggy's ma – the daughter she prayed for she finally loses.

DellaMirandola Add me to those who think Kitty is starting to realise *something* is up with Sal, but not necessarily that he's gay. Would she really consider it a serious possibility? I think this relationship is so beautifully done – we feel for Sal, both in the developing storyline about his career frustrations (carried over from last week where he wasn't invited to Roger's party though he's been there longer than Ken and Pete) and his growing frustrations about his sexuality. But we also get to feel for Kitty, an innocent who is in love with Sal.

Insomniac56 I've seen scenes like that before, but never played with this much control or this depressing an effect. What's interesting is the way Matt Weiner sits on his characters and doesn't allow them full catharsis. In Brokeback Mountain, Michelle Williams was allowed to scream and shout and throw frying pans around when she found out Heath Ledger was making out with Jake Gyllenhall. No such luck for Mrs Sal, who just has to smile, say something nice and quake with quiet terror as she realises why her husband won't sleep with her. Does she even have the language to understand what she's just seen?

EPISODE FIVE: The Fog

"It was all a fog." BETTY

Rather than the London Fog raincoats from Baltimore, this Fog refers to Betty's druggy haze as she gives birth. As Don sits swigging Johnnie Walker and ripping out ads in the waiting room, poor Betty is begging for her husband while the midwife plies her with drugs. We go with her into a David Lynch-style dream where first she crushes a caterpillar in her palm and another where she meets her dead parents in her kitchen as

Gene clutches a mop full of blood. Having Ryan Cutrona actually playing the cleaner in the non-dream scene was also a nice link back to a similar effect with January Jones playing an LA blonde in The Jet Set.

The first dream can be analysed a number of ways (see Thoughts From The Typing Pool below) – is she the insect that's been crushed before she can blossom into a butterfly? The second with her parents telling her to stay within her ambitions ("You're a housecat") seemed fairly straight, besides the odd presence of Medger Evers (see below) – "You see what happens when people speak up?" warns Betty's mother.

Don, meanwhile, meets Sing-Sing guard Dennis in the waiting room. Dennis, we imagine, is the kind of straight up guy Dick Whitman may have turned out like. Dennis's fishing for questions about his job was quite charming – and Don is willing to play ball – but the key exchange comes with Dennis voicing his concerns about the birth: if his wife died, how could he love the baby? Ask Don … When Dennis ignores him later on, you almost wonder if their exchange really happened.

"There's definitely something going on." PRYCE

Evers – a civil rights activist murdered in Mississippi on 12 June – is referenced at various points tonight. Sally had been asking her teacher Miss Farrell about him and it was his funeral on the news in the waiting room.

While the Evers references are pretty subtle, the story with Pete and Admiral was intentionally less so. Pete's pitch to build their base in African-American markets made sense. In fact, I looked at a 1963 copy of Ebony, and Sterling Cooper were already behind media buyers from the more right on firms. But Sterling Cooper is a conservative company. As, it appears, is Admiral – whose men seem offended by the idea of their brand becoming a black one. Even if it makes more money. Years later fashion brands such as Adidas and Tommy Hilfiger were basing their entire brands around appealing to young urban black men to cash in on their cool.

A more revealing exchange is the one between Campbell and Hollis. Piqued by the fact that Pete tries to link his race with the motivation behind his purchase of consumer goods, Hollis turns the tables exquisitely on Pete – referring to the war outside ("We've got bigger problems to think about than a TV") and putting him in his place when Pete says, "It's just Hollis and..." by finishing his sentence with "Mr Campbell."

One take here is that Weiner was juxtaposing two strands of civil rights – the struggle in the south with the more benign assimilation (or lack) of black people into US business and mainstream culture. Doing this shows that the metaphorical boundaries in New York are just as strong as the physical ones down south. Pete's intentions (despite being motivated by business) are, I think, good – he's equating equality with opportunity. But he's from another world to Hollis and it's no surprise that he lacks nuance. There's more to come on this, undoubtedly.

NOTES

- The minor flirtation between Don and Suzanne (Sally's teacher) seemed to be instigated by her as much as Don. She was slightly drunk when she called the Draper house – had she been building up courage?

- Meanwhile Sally – for want of a loving parent – seems to have been confiding in Ms Farrell, as Suzanne knew Betty's dad was Grandpa Gene.

- Duck is back. One suspects that Pete would have been more open to his Grey job offer if it was just he who was asked. "You two have a secret relationship" was a great line too.

- Lift attendant Hollis: "Every job has its ups and downs."

- Cosgrove admiring his new watch: "What time is it? What time *isn't* it?"

CULTURE WATCH

- The music played out over Betty's "fog" was Me Voy a Morir de Amor from Alberto Iglesias's score to Sex And Lucia.

- Betty's errant obstetrician was having dinner at legendary Manhattan Italian restaurant Mamma Leone's.

- Sally's teacher Suzanne Farrell shares a name with the noted ballerina. Elisabeth Moss studied ballet with the real Farrell.

THOUGHTS FROM THE TYPING POOL

RockNRollMassacre The Pete Campbell/Hollis storyline definitely held the most interest, particularly their "reconciliation" at the end of the lift scene. It was difficult to say whether Hollis had genuinely forgiven/moved on from Campbell's insensitive remarks or whether he was again playing the role of subservient elevator boy: I fall slightly on the side of forgiveness with Hollis recognising that Campbell is at least more liberal than most of his peers. Notwithstanding his uncomfortable terminology, Campbell's very conception of *integrated* advertising (rather than advertising simply directed at a single racial group) suggests that this is beyond him simply seeing the economic potential of an emerging market, but being quite spectacularly open minded.

Superspartan Perhaps as well as revealing himself as more liberal Pete is also revealing himself as human after all. Like anyone else would, he's just reluctant to leave a conversation with someone he's got no grudge against on bad terms. Perhaps it's just in situations in which he's trying to impress that he gets it so badly wrong.

Insomniac506 It's extraordinary to consider that Sterling Cooper (and big business in the US generally) couldn't even think of the black community as a legitimate enough group to even be bothered to exploit for marketing purposes. As Lane rather naively intones: "There is something happening."

Promethea I think this ties in with Medgar Evers, a fairly mainstream (though very brave) civil rights leader like King. Pete – who is capitalist through and through – is the kind of person they hoped they could make a deal with, that they could literally talk to (like the Kennedys, perhaps). He's not got the jargon or the liberal background like Paul, but despite the latter's black girlfriend and supposed participation in the Freedom Rides, he may actually be more open to equality rather than lipservice.

Digit I thought the caterpillar [in the dream] was the child and Betty's initial expression of delight was about being able to crush it, which I think she did. This fits with her anger before the dream and with intimations of her buried anger from previous series: the smashed up chair, the shooting.

Exiv96 From what I could see, the advert that Don ripped out while in the waiting room was for Pontiac. In a decade when illustration was supplanted by photography (as Sal lamented in a previous episode), Pontiac's ads continued to be drawn by a duo of illustrators, Art Fitzpatrick and Van Kaufmann, who became known for their glamourous, jet-set themed artworks.

JoeDoone When Dennis Hobart, the Sing-Sing guard, frets about the birth of his baby harming his wife, Don tells him: "Our worst fears lie in anticipation." This is an echo of what Sal told the London Fog people in Baltimore in the first episode. Don, on that occasion, says that change is neither good nor bad in itself, that you can either sulk about it or you can welcome it with a dance, and we see his appreciation of Suzanne's dancing around the maypole. When Don next sees Hobart, the latter's sullen reaction suggests that his worst fears may have been realised to some extent; there is no longer much hope of his becoming "a better man."

Digit I thought Don, seeing Dennis's depth of feeling about his wife was realising unnervingly that he didn't feel the same about Betty. Then there were lots of allusions to Don's fake position: as a matter of fact, he does have a dream of waking up in Sing-Sing; the prison guard knows criminals and can see that Don's an honest guy; and the way all this segued into a discussion of childbirth: "Every one of those animals [inmates] had a mother."

DellaMirandola This episode beautifully focused on Betty and rendered her comprehensible and therefore pitiful. For instance, her sitting in the wheelchair in the hospital corridor while the nurse is on the phone, trying to suppress her labour pains because it wouldn't be nice to let herself go in public. They really did manage to convey the awfulness of the sterile medical world of 1960s hospital births without actually showing us very much awfulness – it was all in the nurses' dialogue.

Insomniac506 Betty standing at the window of the hospital was a beautiful image, waving at her children standing below. It's the perfect 1950s image of motherhood – or at least, an image of motherhood that Betty wants herself to project. After telling Don "I need to put my face on," she's brushed her hair, put on her makeup and is picture perfect at the window with babe in arms, like the Madonna. There's also a pane of glass separating her from her family and the rest of the world, which is pretty much everything you need to know about Betty.

Dominia I was also touched by Betty, who somehow comes through the pain and humiliation of the birth holding her new baby quite tenderly, and a little reluctant to surrender him at home, watching him anxiously and protectively. And what an ending moment, maternal instincts fully functioning albeit on auto-pilot as she rises from sleep to go to her crying baby. Surely Sally's glowing face as she greets her mother is sign enough that we should soften a little bit towards her.

Mad Men & The Movies

Mad Men's bound up but distant relationship with cinema

DANNY LEIGH

Matthew Weiner's sleekly seductive portrait of a drink-sodden early 60s New York advertising agency has, of course, now secured an ardent following even among those who were at first wary of it – and in the spirit of full disclosure I'll happily admit I'm one such sceptic turned true believer. Which is why I found my brow furrowing at an article which put forward the opinion that the show's vision of the Camelot era is excessively "dour", as if timeless inner turmoil might be magically spirited away by a vague general mood of gleaming optimism. But none the less, it's was a valuable piece because not looking at Don and Betty Draper as at least partly cinematic creations is to miss much of what makes them so alluring.

It's a relationship that's often intrigued me during the rise of the multi-episode format that's so efficiently nicked at least a chunk of cinema's core audience. The Sopranos, of course, was tied hand and bloodied foot to the movies, its doughy Mafiosi obsessed with Cagney and The Godfather, creator David Chase's esteem for cinema as the "higher" art form forever informing the show's identity. The Wire, on the other hand, never appeared nearly as indebted to film, its flavour drawn instead from non-fiction reportage and David Simon's own previous TV work on Homicide: Life on the Street. But Mad Men's gorgeous, bleak worldview is, fittingly for a project that's made ambivalence its keystone, at once bound up with the movies and strangely distant from them.

Certainly, on-screen, there's precious little of the film buffery that inspired such golden Soprano moments as Christopher's encounter with Ben Kingsley – for the most part only the death of Marilyn registered as more than a blip in the characters' routine. And yet the film culture of the time is always there in the aura of the show, the rat pack snazz of the original Ocean's Eleven and the brightly coloured idyll of A Hole in the Head (its Doris Day-sung theme song High Hopes doubling as a JFK campaign anthem) swirling about every episode like a mass of cigarette smoke, central to the idea of America the series' characters are both forever parcelling up for sale in their ad campaigns and falling for in their own fractured lives.

Almost any of Douglas Sirk's grand and beautiful Hollywood tragedies could, of course, be thrown into the mix, and Imitation of Life is the grandest and most beautiful of them all. Elsewhere, it's a big check for The Best of Everything and Advise and Consent too, but I'd also throw in another candidate – The Sweet Smell of Success, a little early having come out in '57, true, but in its hellishly neon-lit Manhattan and scuttling press agent Sidney Falco a fascinating counterpoint to the superficially sanitised ad men of Stirling Cooper.

Then there's Hitchcock – another whose most relevant work (Vertigo, Notorious) would have been in the past for Don and Betty, but whose influence often seems inescapable watching the show. I would at this point direct you to a fine video essay at Film Freak Central (bit.ly/madmenhitchcock) that pinpoints all manner of homages to the man, from the choice of camera angles to, of course, the Kim Novak-esque treatment of ice-blonde star January Jones.

And yet, for we scruffy souls watching in 2009, it's also hard not to feel the impeccably coiffed presence of David Lynch, who at the time the series is set would have been a teenage Eagle Scout – and who then embarked on a career's worth of movies that remain psychically connected with that same era even now, from the picket-fence fantasia of Blue Velvet to the

Locomotion of Inland Empire. At once bound up with the past and pointed at the future, the links between Mad Men and the movies are plentiful – and more than just a parade of great suits. Although they are, of course, really great suits…

EPISODE SIX: Guy Walks Into An Advertising Agency

"The Doctor said he'd never golf again." POWELL

Considering that the Brits from PPL were unsubtly using the Independence Day holidays to restructure the office, it is fitting that this week's episode nearly turns into an Ealing farce. Pryce's replacement-to-be, Guy Mackendrick (Cantab, LSE) has his foot mown off by Lois driving a mini John Deere that Ken had triumphantly brought into the office. Mackendrick – a smarmy Don 2.0 in his grey suit – has been airlifted in by PPL to replace the efficient, if not stellar Lane Pryce. Don's "who is this kid?" look is, however, quickly removed. Especially as he realises he will be reporting to Guy and that Bert's hints about PPL taking Don to London can't be true. (In fact, this may have been a canny tactic aimed at reuniting them.)

So Don, along with Pryce – who's been told to run the Bombay office – are relieved when the young upstart is ruthlessly cast aside in the accident. The grisly shots of Paul and Harry getting sprayed with blood and Lois driving slowly straight through a glass wall would have been disturbing if they weren't so out of the show's character and very funny to boot. Having nearly been excommunicated by the reshuffle, Roger proves his worth in the accident's aftermath, strolling smugly into the office ("Jesus, it's like Iwo Jima out there!") and reassuring those who might be at fault for the accident – "Believe me, somewhere in this business, this has happened before." He, like Don and Lane has had his kingdom secured (for now) by the accident. Deus ex mowing machine and all that.

"I'm really happy that you got what you wanted." PEGGY

Less amusing, however, was Joan's valedictory party being overshadowed by the Brits and, more so, her husband Greg not getting his residency as a surgeon. Despite previous events, Joan does seem to genuinely love Greg and is more upset for him than angry at his selfishness in not calling. Or is she just fooling herself? "I married you for your heart, not your hands," she reassures him as he broods in his scrubs of failure. Presuming that she really wants to, she'll now have to wait to leave work and start a family or move to Alabama. And Huntsville don't seem no place for a Joan Holloway. Either way, she hasn't got – as Peggy presumes of both her and Don – everything she wants. Speaking of which, Joan and Don's embrace at the hospital was another touching moment, with a wonderful payoff: "One minute you're on top of the the world, the next some secretary is running you over with a lawnmower."

We don't know as yet if Joan will be able to go back to Sterling Cooper. If not, her main legacy at Sterling Cooper could well be her patronage of Peggy – who lies slightly (only slightly) on the easier side of 21st century women's advancement. For what it's worth, we wish her "caviar and children" too.

NOTES

- I loved Hooker jokingly telling the increasingly pompous guitar-wielding rebel of Madison Avenue, Paul Kinsey, to shave his beard – and his serious response: "Who the hell are you people?!"

- Another good laugh came with Harry clapping by himself in the conference room – and not realising he was being promoted.

- Are (were?) Pete's days numbered? "Account management – that's Mr Cosgrove … and Mr Campbell for the present."

- Another funny moment came with Don dropping Sally's doll

back off in her room after she'd chucked it out of the window – only for Sally to think her evil baby brother has summoned it back. Sally does, however, finally get a hug (and some affection) from her folks as they realise that she's not jealous of Eugene, just scared that he's her grandpa reincarnate.

- Don, for once, seems intimidated when he realises that Connie from the party is Connie Hilton. He still holds it together well enough to play a little hardball.

20TH CENTURY TALES

- Joan's slightly erroneous mocking about Profumo ("We could hire some prostitutes, I know your prime minister enjoys them") raised a smile.

- We got (I think) the first reference to Vietnam as young copywriter Dale reveals his draft worries.

CULTURE WATCH

- Dale channels The Beverly Hillbillies when he says to Ken: "Listen, Mr Clampett, you better get your iron horse out of reception."

- The credits play out to Dylan's Song To Woody. Dylan – like Don – came from the Midwest, changed his identity and became a superstar. The song during the party, meanwhile, was Jody Reynolds' Come On Twist.

- Lane has been reading Twain, and Roger summons up the ghost of Paul Revere in his comment: "The British are coming!".

- Bert refers to Don and Roger as his Lewis and Martin – a reference to Jerry Lewis and Dean Martin's early career as a comic pair.

THOUGHTS FROM THE TYPING POOL

PureImagination This was Joan's episode. I loved that she was so competent after the accident, proving that (unlike her husband) she is a natural medic. I am cringing with embarassment at the idea she might have to go back to Sterling Cooper and admit that Greg didn't get the residency and there are no babies and caviar. Surely she would rather move to Alabama than do that?

Digit What genius this foot business. Where else has this much pain, blood and permanent mutilation ever been so funny? You have to go back to season one with Roger's epic projectile vomit in the lobby to see the Sterling Cooper offices being anywhere near as inappropriately splatted before. There are many reasons to want Guy Mackendrick out of the way, it's like some cosmic Murder on the Orient Express. Everyone had a motive, so the stars just went into alignment. For me, the actor's dreadful accent was reason enough to take him out, but was also glad of Lane's reprieve from his roundly unjust banishment to the colonies. Among the coldly sadistic Brit caricatures, he's the one turning out human.

PureImagination Would it be too obvious to say that in Song to Woody "I'm seein' your world of people and things, Your paupers and peasants and princes and kings," is likely to refer to the visiting Brits?

Of course the biggest and most obvious metaphor in the song is about a new world being born. In the last few episodes there's been a growing sense that the world of MM is on its way out – most obviously at Roger's party, and in Pete's inability to understand why a client wouldn't want more black customers. In this episode we had our first Vietnam reference and when the Dylan song came on I was slightly jolted because the end credit music so far has been very 1950s and smooth. Another sign that the times they are a-changing?

Dominia The Sally scenes were both moving and interesting as a contrast between parenting styles. Kudos to Betty for genuinely trying, but she's still too frozen or immature to understand the difference between genuine love and affection and buying it with gifts.

DellaMirandola The juxtaposition of Joan and Betty, being wife and mother according to the 1950s Handbook For The Little Woman, was nicely done: Joan saying all the lines from How To Support Your Husband and Betty all the lines from Is Your Child Jealous Of A New Baby. But in each case it didn't quite work – does Joan really believe that she married Greg for his heart, not his medical skills? Betty's case was more complicated: she was at her best this episode – the scene with Don in the kitchen where they seemed really to be a happily married couple for about five minutes – and there is no right or wrong answer to the question about baby Gene. Should Betty really be so unselfish that her husband's dislike of her late father, or her daughter's childish anxieties, should really trump her wanting to remember Gene by calling the new baby after him?

CrashBoomBang One of the many great things about Mad Men is that while it's set in the past it is really about how we are now – how we got here, how we are different and often suprisingly not that different from just two generations back. The theme of judging by appearances – race, gender, class and attractiveness, the role of image and posing and how this related to consumption and politics, with violence, betrayal and fear always lurking, is so contemporary.

The conversation Peggy had with Don last week asking for a raise struck me because I had an almost identical conversation with a male boss about two years ago. Perhaps Don was more surprised/sardonic about the idea of equal pay, but the brush off (we can't afford it) was exactly the same. 50 years of progress.

EPISODE SEVEN: Seven Twenty Three

"They want me, but they can't have me." DON

Seven Twenty Three is a case of two whodunits: who did Peggy sleep with? And why was Don out cold on the floor? The fiddling with the narrative enlivened an episode that while good, perhaps existed to set up a lot of the action for the second half of the series.

Don, as we know, is not a man who likes being tied down by a contract. But as Connie Hilton – after a nervy chat – offers him his NYC hotels, Draper finds himself staring down the ink barrel. Eventually he signs it as Cooper uses some old persuasion tactics (ie, he knows Dick Whitman – how long has he been saving that one?) and Don is now tied, for three years, to the company store.

The whodunit involves Don's little misadventure with hitchhiking newlyweds-to-be/con artists Sandy and Doug who drug Draper with two phenobarbitals before taking his cash. More important was Don's hallucination (similar to Betty's a fortnight ago) in which his guilt (for tonight, for always) manifests itself in a vision of his father telling bawdy jokes and calling him a bum – "What do you make? You grow bullshit." We often forget that underneath that grey suit there's a scared heart beating and waiting to be found out.

Finally, I liked the directorial touch of having Cooper and Hilton both sit in Don's chair at the desk. He may have a gang of sycophants hovering outside clapping him, but these two men aren't afraid to remind him of his place.

"We all have skills we don't use." BETTY

Don might have Connie Hilton, but Betty also has a new older man in her life. Having been made secretary of her Junior League group, she is asked to help stop the demolition of a reservoir. She, like us, remembers Henry Francis – the stomach toucher from Roger's party. His immediate call back after she leaves him a message suggests he's been thinking about her and so it proves – their meeting over coffee about the reservoir is loaded with subtext. We know that ice-cool Betty is keen too, and she confirms it with the purchase of the antique fainting couch ("for ladies who got overwhelmed"), ruining the feng shui of her newly designed front room.

Don is obviously older than Betty, Henry is even older. He's handsome of course but is it a leap too far to suggest a hint of Electra complex in a still-mourning Betty's admiration for Henry? Looks like we'll be seeing more of the Republican strategist anyway.

"You're good, get better, stop asking for things." DON

Peggy's whodunit was more clearly signposted than Don's. On first watch, it was only when she walked into Duck's suite that it's clear that he is the man in the bed. But on second viewing there are clues throughout: the Hermès scarf, the shots of Duck's meetings in a hotel. Nevertheless it came out of nowhere. Has she cheapened her position by sleeping with Duck? She had already said no to a job at Grey before kissing him, so maybe it's harmless fun. Unlike Duck's sweet talk: "I'm going to give you a go around like you've never had." Yuk.

Perhaps Peggy accepts Phillips' advances as a result of low self-esteem, following the yelling she takes from Don. Don was obviously harsh, and his contract chat with Roger leads to him lashing out at Peggy, but is he right? Does she need to put her head down for a couple of years and learn (he takes a similar tone with Pete after all) or is it more "know your place, woman"? You suspect the former.

NOTES

- The eclipse they're watching is the total solar eclipse of 20 July 1963.

- A rare mistake? The Betty Crocker cookbook in the Drapers' kitchen wasn't published until 1967.

- Don and Suzanne's serious talk of philandering men was made hilarious by everyone else in the scene having their heads stuck in boxes. An apt metaphor for many of Ossining's married couples.

20TH CENTURY TALES

- More Vietnam. Pete discusses a friend who's working at Secretary of Defence Robert McNamara's office who knows that North American are getting huge orders for military hardware.

- Doug is apparently trying to avoid the draft by marrying. He describes himself as "1A, unmarried" which is the most available category of men in the draft order.

- Bert on Hilton: "I met him once, he's a bit of an eccentric isn't he?"

CULTURE WATCH

- Don signed his name under an address for Bullet Park Road. There is no real road in Ossining of course, but Bullet Park is the wonderful – very Mad Men – novel by John Cheever set in Ossining.

- Sixteen Tons was a great choice of song after Don signed his soul "to the company store".

- Peggy is reading Conrad Hilton's book Be My Guest which recounts his rise from owning one hotel in a dusty Texas oil town to becoming one of the world's most prominent hoteliers.

- Roger has been asked to provide a quote for Ogilvy's Confessions Of An Ad Man. Or, as he would have it: "It should be called 1,000 reasons I'm so great." Ho-Ho mentioned reading the Ogilvy book in episode four.

THOUGHTS FROM THE TYPING POOL

DogManStar Clearly, Matthew Weiner is a believer in David Simon's dictum "fuck the casual viewer". Pete's revealing of Don's secret to Cooper at the end of the first season is now used as a weapon by Cooper against Don.

JoeDoone Don is now more chained down than he has been in a long time; what Cooper knows has been hanging like a cheque waiting to be cashed. Don wants to be free, he wants to be different – he doesn't like the teacher writing him off as a cookie-cutter local wanting his wicked way with her.

Maceasy The crucial line was when Don snarled at Betty that she didn't understand business, that not having a contract was about retaining power and having control over the situation. By relinquishing at the end, he only symbolized what had happened already in the episode

Insomniac506 Don is being forced out of his comfort zones. He has not one, but two alpha males – Connie and Cooper – sitting in his office chair giving him advice this week. The schoolteacher sees through his facade and manages to dodge his continual statements that nothing's happening. And then of course there's the ambush about signing the contract, Betty's cucumber-cool interrogation ("What's the matter, you don't know where you're going to be in three years?") AND being drugged up and robbed by a white trash teen trash couple and left bleeding in a hotel room. I'd say Don's hermetically sealed universe is about to split apart, big time. Look at how much talking he has to do in this episode, and the number of confrontations he launches into – at Connie, at Sterling and Cooper, at Peggy, at Betty, at the schoolteacher and at his nightmare vision of his hillbilly daddy.

KeithyD Culture watch addendum: The lady at the Junior League meeting mentioned Silent Spring as background to their concern about the new development. Rachel Carson's book kicked off the environmental movement, and was published in

September of 1962, so was a big thing by the time of this episode, July 1963.

Smee Peggy going to see Duck was clearly a reaction to her confrontation with Don, but I'm not sure that sleeping with him was. It was a nice hotel room, he's older than the clueless man-boys she's been with before, and having no ties and being a little upset, all those compliments probably felt quite nice – although Duck's chat up line nearly made me vomit.

PureImagination Don's dressing down of Peggy was blatantly unfair, especially when you consider she hasn't asked for anything else except fair pay. If you consider that he kept Pete's conversation professional and completely encouraging, and then made Peggy's so horribly personal, with the stinging "there's not one thing you've done here that I couldn't live without". An especially bad show considering that Peggy had done the groundwork and read Hilton's book when Pete didn't even know he'd written one.

Insomniac506 Another detail in the scripting that I really appreciated was when Doug said that although he didn't want to be conscripted, he also didn't want to offend Don if Don had "served". I found that moment touching, as it reflected the deference and respect that Americans were still showing to war veterans in the 1960s, in the pre-Vietnam era. Don's generation was perhaps the last one in American society to receive that kind of unambiguous hero worship.

DellaMirandola The juxtaposition of Suzanne and Henry is interesting: Suzanne the tell-it-like-it-is flower child appeals to Don, while Betty is drawn to someone who has all the trappings of power and status, and who shares her interest in beautiful material possessions. But also Suzanne piques Don's interest by both displaying her physical attraction and holding back mentally: women telling him what's wrong with him always seem to attract Don. Betty, on the other hand, is attracted to someone who displays interest in her as a person – the one thing she never seems to get from Don. Henry may recommend the fainting couch to her, but he also expects to have an adult discussion with her as Junior League spokeswoman.

EPISODE EIGHT: Souvenir

"You're going to have a lot of first kisses." BETTY

With Don being dragged around the world by Hilton, "Birdie" is given a chance to escape her cage as Betty slips off to join him *a Roma* for two days. As well as being an anthropology grad, Betty speaks Italian (having modelled there) and we almost immediately meet a different woman to Ossining Betty. Their reasons for being in Lazio are, of course, influenced by Henry. Having used his position to help the Junior Leaguers' campaign at the town hall, he makes it clear that he's doing so just to please Betty. After they share a kiss, a combination of guilt and twinging hormones make her decide to leave the kids with Carla and go to Italy.

There we see Betty as she presumably was in Manhattan: wickedly flirting with young men, indulging her beauty salon whims, looking like a Guido Anselmi fantasy in 8½ – which was released summer 1963, incidentally. This is the life she might be leading without her "old and ugly" husband. The scene with Betty speaking in Italian with the two men even leads to Don, for once, not being in on the joke.

Betty is obviously unhappy with her life (she sounds like Revolutionary Road's April Wheeler when she tells Don "I hate this place, I hate our friends, I hate this town"). The Rome trip for her is almost like an affair. She doesn't want sneaky kisses in the car park, she wants to be whisked away to the Eternal City, to order room service and put her hair up. Whether she'll do anything with Henry remains to be seen, but for now Don will have to do. If their life was like this all the time, she may even be happy but as soon as she reenters her suburban prison the frostiness returns. Although, it must be noted that she is much sweeter to Sally these days – the two shared a lovely wordless lipstick moment at the mirror and the chat in which Betty tells her daughter (wink, nudge) "I don't want you going around kissing boys" was wonderful.

This episode is called Souvenir, ie the gold colosseum trinket that Don gives Betty, but the trip itself was a souvenir of a different life.

"You always get that guilty look on your face when we see little children." TRUDY

While Betty joins Don on his trip, Pete is home alone, watching kids' TV after Trudy heads off for a week (presumably with her parents – hence no Pete as he fell out with Trudy's father in 1962). He's so bored that he offers to help his next-door neighbour's nanny Gudrun after she spills wine on an expensive dress. Is this an act of altruism aimed at relieving his malaise?

This being Pete, of course, he doesn't have it in him to just do the right thing. After heading to Bonwit Teller to get the dress replaced and meeting a none-too-thrilled-to-see-him Joan, who's moonlighting as a retail manager (see Notes), Pete returns the dress – hoping to share a stein or two with the au pair. A rejection and an armful of drinks later he tries his luck again; while she doesn't say no, it's a disturbing, not-quite-consensual turn of events. So much so that the next day Ed Lawrence has to tell him to stay away from the women in the building. Every time you think he's grown …

There follows an odd couple of scenes in which Pete nearly confesses to his infidelity and then (possibly) tacitly confesses/ tries to transfer blame onto Trudy when he tells her "I don't want you to go away anymore without me", ie, it's not his fault if he can't control his urges with no wife around to sate his desires.

NOTES

- Plenty of Hermès placement in Joan's store. Joan looks upset that the veneer on her decision to leave and be Greg's housewife is cracking. Fortunately, Pete is too busy struggling to make smalltalk to even register her position – if he cares at all. She also reveals that her abusive husband Greg is going to be a psychiatrist.

- After leaving Carla with their tiny baby (and Francine's kids), Betty and Don don't even have the goodwill to say thank you afterwards.

- "They should pay you for this." Another class tic. Don doesn't understand Betty's volunteerism. He also blithely scrawls his flight details on the calling list she is using.

- Betty's nimbyism: "They should just do it up in Newburgh, it's already disgusting."

- One of the ways the production designers created Rome was to use the Dorothy Chandler Pavilion in LA to recreate the Rome Hilton.

- Pete's still reading Ebony, despite his bollocking.

CULTURE WATCH

- The end credit music was There's A Small Hotel by Richard Rodgers performed by Bobby Van and Kay Coulter from the musical On Your Toes.

- Pete is watching stop-motion Christian kids' TV show Davey and Goliath.

THOUGHTS FROM THE TYPING POOL

JJ139 Sorry, but I think Pete raped the au pair, there was nothing consensual about it, the poor girl had to let him in because she was beholden to him for replacing the dress. He then took advantage. The neighbour knew for sure, but being 1960s there is no way a WASP like Pete would go down for raping a foreign au pair. Even in the past year, look how the American public and media viewed the Amanda Knox case in Italy.

Bella79 I wouldn't agree, though, that his confession to Trudy was putting the blame on her; Pete's never been able to properly comprehend what he is feeling, and so while he knew he felt guilty the only way he had to vocalise it was to phrase it in the way he did. Kartheiser played Pete's confused guilt perfectly.

Dominia The most interesting theme here is sex and power, especially in the contrast between how Betty and Gudrun handle it. Gudrun tries to reject the bargain offered by Pete, and then to refuse "payment", but when he bangs on her door again finally capitulates (with some ambiguity). She's a victim, without blame, especially as Pete has double power over her with the dress and his being alpha male. Betty on the other hand is really learning how to use and enjoy her sexual power. I found it really interesting and quite impressive that she was obviously toying with the idea of taking things further with Henry, then intelligently chose the more glamorous as well as virtuous option, a weekend in Rome with Don, where she can also enjoy flirting with the natives – in front of him.

DellaMirandola There is a clear echo in Pete's behaviour here of his behaviour with Peggy in the very first episode – he meets an innocent young woman to whom he, for some reason already feeling emasculated and childlike, feels superior; he gets to play the man with her by offering advice; he gets drunk and turns up on her doorstep wanting sex. Then we're shown her letting him come in to her flat, but it's left unclear what actually went on. Obviously he was using the sense of his being in a powerful position to her to demand sex, but we don't see whether he physically forced himself on her or not. We were shown Dr Greg really forcing himself on Joan against her will. So if they had wanted to put Pete in the same category, they would have shown that, yes? Instead they faded out on what I saw as passive acquiescence (which is hardly "yes please" but is it rape?).

Discussant All this talk about Peter raping the au pair misses the point: none of the participants in the incident – neither Pete, the au pair, nor the au pair's employer – would have conceived of it as rape, just as Joan did not conceive of her experience as rape. The power imbalances illuminated by feminism were so murky and unnamed at the time that it would all have fallen under the category of "seduction".

Insomniac506 This is the difficulty of trying to judge the morality of Mad Men by our contemporary post-feminist standards. It's fairly clear that Weiner is aware of these differences in 1960s vs modern morality, and he seems to like writing and directing scenes that will throw up that kind of discomfort. The horror of watching the Drapers throw litter away in a park, Betty smoking like a train during her pregnancy and so on. It was only 40ish years ago, and yet it might as well be science fiction.

I especially appreciate how Weiner just presents this behaviour and lets the audience sit with the discomfort this creates, rather than reassuring us by adding a contemporary response that would be out of place. He isn't tempted to put late 20th century expressions into the heads and mouths of characters from the early 1960s. MM doesn't glamorise this behaviour – if anything, the show is very revealing (in very subtle ways) about the damage caused to the characters – but he lets the action play out as it would have done in the early 1960s.

Mad Men shows the morality of another age without condescending to it. We may think that we're more enlightened than the folk of Sterling Cooper, but the show reminds us that those people thought of themselves, at the time, as the most clever, the most enlightened and the most successful people in the world. It reminds us that in 50 years time, people will be making drama about the early 2000s and laughing at the antiquated sensibilities of our supposedly superior age.

EPISODE NINE: Wee Small Hours

"By golly, I'm King Midas." CONRAD HILTON

Don Draper is losing his edge. Hilton is dragging him around town and calling him at home in the middle of the night, his work is suffering, his wife is trying to start her own romance and he's finally made a move for Suzanne.

But first, Hilton. The pair seem like kindred souls and Hilton confirms it when, while discussing his ideas for empire building, he tells Don: "You're my angel … you're like a son. In fact, you're more than that. Because you didn't have what they have, you understand." Don's acquiescence to his demands suggests that the feeling is somewhat mutual but any chumminess is quickly cast aside when Hilton rebuffs Sterling Cooper's ideas for ignoring his Hilton On The Moon suggestions. Hilton is the kind of son-of-a-bitch father one imagines Don – rather than Dick – would have had. And he, like Don, has everything and nothing at the same time.

Hilton's neediness does, however, give Don a chance to leave the house – he goes in early to write a brief and bumps into Suzanne Farrell, who is out running. A rebuttal first time around leads to a late night dash to her apartment to woo her. With Betty at home and Suzanne away, Don's not so much having his cake and eating it as having his steak and flame-grilling it. As Suzanne – who understands his desires – warns him, it's a disaster waiting to happen. But like Rachel, Midge and so many others before him, she seems unable to resist.

Meanwhile Betty is dipping (rather than plunging) her toes into the extramarital water via a coy letter exchange with Henry. This leads to Henry arriving at the Drapers' and Betty being forced to put on a Republican fundraiser (for the doomed Rockefeller) in order to steer off a suspicious Carla. When Henry sends a female advisor to speak in his place, Mrs Draper indulges her inner-teenager and drives straight to Albany in order to throw the collection tin at him. She can't however quite go through with her desires – and calls their kissing in his office "tawdry". She needs to learn some tips from her husband.

"Watch your tongue young man. Carla works for me, not you." BETTY

Mad Men's handling of the Civil Rights situation in 1963 has been as subtle as its cinematography. Tonight's episode contained the most obvious nods. Firstly we hear Suzanne tell Don that she's going to read the I Have A Dream Speech to the kids – who need an adult to confirm to them that MLK is right. Suzanne is paying attention, unlike Don's wife. Betty's white indifference plays a key part in two scenes. The first is wonderfully framed: Betty and her friends discuss how uncivilised segregation is, while in the back of the shot we see Carla, dressed in her maid's outfit, answering a doorbell ignored by everyone else, before meekly taking away Betty's tray. We think that Betty gets it after a visibly upset Carla turns off the radio, with news of the 16th Street Bombing (in which four young girls were killed in an explosion at a church Birmingham, Alabama). "You can leave it on your station," she tells Carla before asking her if she's alright. Then she follows it with the callous: "It's really made me wonder about Civil Rights, maybe it's not supposed to happen right now?" There's a long way to go yet.

"I got it. You're at work." LEE GARNER JR

Sal's Baltimore indiscretion finally catches up with him as Lee Garner Jr from Lucky Strike makes a pass at him. After Sal turns him down, a vindictive Garner instructs the inept Harry to get rid of Sal. Crane's reluctance to do so means the task is left to Roger after Garner storms out upon seeing Sal. But Don, swayed by what he saw in Maryland, thinks it was Romano hitting on

Garner (there were echoes of Betty to Jimmy in series two in Don's "You people") and has little hesitation in agreeing with Roger's decision. We later see Sal on what appears to be the set of a Village People video phoning Kitty to tell her not wait up. A heartbreaking end to Sal's career at Sterling Cooper.

20TH CENTURY TALES

- Connie tells Don: "New York City is not a domestic destination, like say Dallas." Dallas was mentioned in the last episode too. It's like they know what's coming.

- Hilton/Don's assertion that "America is wherever we look and wherever we're going to be" foreshadows the future and current bouts of globalisation and Americanisation that defined the 20th century. "It's my purpose in life to bring America to the world, whether they like it or not." Nice that he still has some prohibition booze left though.

- Along with MLK's speech, Don's radio is broadcasting news about two murders in the Upper East Side. The Career Girl Murders, as they became known, witnessed the killing of Newsweek researcher Janice Wylie, 21, and schoolteacher Emily Hoffert, 23. The accused, George Whitmore Jr, was a black American with a low IQ who was beaten and near-framed by the NYPD and DA's office.

CULTURE WATCH

- Harry's mother in law thinks he looks like Perry Mason. As Kinsey kindly tells him: "It's not a compliment, she thinks you're fat."

- Matthew Weiner told Abigail Spencer to listen to Leonard Cohen's Suzanne to get into character.

- At one point Hilton stands in front of Titian's Noli Me Tangere – "Don't touch me".

- No actual Laughing Lennie in the soundtrack but we were

played out to Duke Ellington's Prelude To A Kiss performed by Nnenna Freelon.

THOUGHTS FROM THE TYPING POOL

RockNRollMassacre Carla's stoical silence while listening to the radio broadcast of the Birmingham bomb funerals must have been one of the most heartrendingly moving scenes Mad Men has portrayed so far. Mad Men presents itself as a prism through which we view the past and often that results in this twisted irony that it becomes easy to forget the immense (to me, unimaginable) pain, conviction and struggle that African-Americans (and women) must have lived with in order to be recognised. To present something that was purely emotional but never sentimental, resulted in one of the most beautiful scenes through the whole three seasons.

Keithy D In Neal Stephenson's Cryptonomicon a character observes that all rich and powerful people are control freaks, something borne out in many different facets in this episode. Connie's belief that he can dominate Don's life; Lee Garner's belief that he can have Sal fired; Betty's wish to have Henry; Don's belief that he can take Suzanne and she should be grateful …

But in the end, perhaps the episode is as much about thwarted desire as anything else. Connie doesn't get his moon; Garner doesn't (immediately) get Sal fired; Betty doesn't have Henry; Don gets Suzanne, but not necessarily on his terms. So maybe there's a subtle subtext – made overt in Hilton's avowed desire to place his hotel all over the globe and even on the moon – that American supremacism (as challenged by Dr King) that says "we want it and we can have it, now" is disputed. The episode shows that they *can't* have it now just because they want it – whatever it is – or if they get it, it might not be what they thought it was.

DogManStar I'm guessing Don's "you people" wasn't a reference to Sal being an Italian American. Though it seemed the subtext from Don was "You should have lain back and thought of Sterling Cooper". It's interesting that Sal's response to being fired was to go cruising. He's clearly liberated from the prospect of living the double life.

Kinetic Sal's sacking was harsh, but in its own way confirms why Mad Men is so different from many US shows. In most shows an injustice will eventually be righted but Mad Men – just like real life – will not necessarily give us that satisfaction and is all the better for it.

SaintSnowy I love the fact that even the minor characters have so much meat on them, like Carla and Suzanne. For example, I like the fact that the self-obsessed Don and Betty finally caught a whiff of the political upheavals going on in the background and in the wider world. Both of them were forced into hearing what was happening on the radio by others, and both of them seemed much less interested in the news, and more interested in who they were with (Don with Suzanne, and Betty with Carla, trying to be nice to her so she wouldn't grass her up to Don, whereas Carla probably has bigger problems to worry about than Betty and her politican boyfriend).

EPISODE TEN: The Colour Blue

"Well he knows how to leave a room." DANNY FARRELL

We knew that Don's veneer is cracking, but tonight we see just how far. After leaving the key to his mystery drawer in his dressing gown, Betty hears it rattling around in the tumble drier (rumbled by the consumer goods – O Fortuna!). She's smiling as she opens Don's chest with it, but the bounty she finds within knocks her off her feet: pictures of Don marked "Dick", a divorce certificate and a bond for a house for Anna Draper and Dick and Don's dog tags.

Fittingly, just as Betty discovers the Whitman family, Don is trying to atone for the death of his brother by reaching out to Suzanne's sibling Danny, who is getting in the way of his affair. Danny seems resigned to failure because of his epilepsy but Suzanne manages to sort him out with a job in Massachusetts. As Don drives him there, he reaches out and encourages him to pull himself up (like Don did) before doing the right thing and letting him go his own way. "I swore to myself I would try and do this right once," he says, as he hands him his card for emergencies – a lifeline he never gave to his own brother Adam.

Little does he know that at home, Betty is riding a wave of anger and waiting to confront him, entirely unaware that Don is betraying her in a different way at Suzanne's. By the time he does return at 5.30pm the next day, she's not got the energy for the battle. At the Sterling Cooper party, there's some wonderful wordless acting from January Jones as she non-listens to Don's speech and thinks: "Who the hell *is* this man?"

The episode is called The Colour Blue and Suzanne and Don's early post-coital chat about perception of colours – "How do I know if what I see as blue is the same as it it to you?" – feeds through to Betty's discovery. She's been seeing Don as "blue" for all these years – but he's a completely different colour.

"Wearing a dress isn't going to help you with Western Union." KINSEY

After her shellacking from Don a few weeks back, Peggy proved her skills as a copywriter tonight and left Paul Kinsey reeling at the same time. Despite having improved the "Paul Kinsey Theatre" Aqua Net idea in front of Don, Paul takes the easy view that Peggy's only got where she is because she's a woman and pits himself against her as they think of Western Union campaigns. While Peggy is diligently committing her ideas to tape – Don-style – Kinsey is getting drunk, looking at his old Playtex non-triumph and listening to jazz to drum up some inspiration. When it does finally strike after a conversation with janitor Achilles ("Achilles, I have thought of something very, very good"), he promptly falls asleep before writing it down.

Thankfully due to a combination of Kinsey's knowledge of Chinese proverbs ("The faintest ink is better than the best memory") and Peggy's ad instincts they produce a great idea together. Kinsey's reaction to Peggy's skill – "By … god" – was perhaps the most gratifying moment of series three.

A final point – I loved Peggy's assumption that "talk to Achilles" was some kind of classical euphemism that went over her head. If only, eh Paul?

"We finally have an answer to the question, what makes Don Draper smile?" LANE PRYCE

A quick note on the potential sale of Sterling Cooper. Only Lane knows so far but PPL are using the 40th anniversary party as a way to advertise the agency to buyers. The chat between the two (literally) disenfranchised ex-owners was rather telling – particularly Cooper's introspection and Roger's growing contempt for the leapfrogging Don.

NOTES

- A triptych of great lines for Lane: "Am I to entertain your ballad of dissatisfaction?"; (On it not being England) "I've been here 10 months and nobody's asked me where I went to school" and (on his big speech) "Churchill rousing? Or Hitler rousing?"

- Poor Jane in the car with Roger's mother. First mistaken for Margaret before Roger is asked … "Does Mona know?"

- What with Suzanne's brother's epilepsy, Guy's foot and Sal's sexuality, Mad Men certainly does a good job of sticking two fingers up to equal-opps/H&S recidivists.

- After the phantom call Sally stage whispers "Jeez, Louise"?

- Don still keeps a supply of dry-cleaned shirts in his office drawer.

- Plenty of great shots: particularly Betty closing the study door before we cut straight to Suzanne opening the front door to let Don in.

CULTURE WATCH

- Betty is reading Mary McCarthy's The Group in the bath. The Group was a frank account of a group of New York women dealing with sex, contraception, and breastfeeding – a world not too far away from Betty's had she stayed in Manhattan one imagines. Indeed Candace Bushnell's Sex And The City was commissioned as a modern version of The Group.

THOUGHTS FROM THE TYPING POOL

JoeDoone The driver who comes to pick up the Draper clan is Chinese, just like the author of the maxim about how "the faintest ink is better than the best memory". The ink on Don's honourable discharge, property deed and divorce papers (the latter instigated by Anna) has wiped out Betty's notion of Don.

RocknRollMassacre [On accusations Mad Men has become a soap opera] This is exactly why it's interesting to me; it's hardly a soap opera. More, the melodrama, strange coincidences and so on are part of an atmosphere which was never realistic, which trades on strange moments of the uncanny. Not only this, but these uncanny coincidences are often playing on real pop culture tropes of the 1950s and 60s – the real pop culture of second rate movies and second rate television soap operas. That it does this without being oh-so-knowing and ironic is what's so fascinating about it. It's post-modernist in the best sense of the word – looking at history, particularly the history of popular culture – and working out how we in the 21st century respond to it, how it continues to shape our attitudes on an intensely personal, kaleidoscopic level and how it shaped the attitudes of people at the time.

Yes, there's some elements of melodrama and ridiculous coincidence, but this has nothing to do with a decline in the standard of the programme, it's far far too intelligent for that. It's all there for a reason, it's part of the whole exploration of our continued aestheticisation of the 60s.

DellaMirandola Didn't Peggy look like she was really enjoying being the Perfect Woman whose immaculate hair makes her the envy of all her friends in Paul Kinsey Theatre? That reminded me of Jackie Kennedy's hairdresser telling the story of how he used to travel around doing makeovers. The number one hair problem of the day was: 'my hair moves in the wind' and hairspray that chained every lock into place was the must-have product. I suppose there is a nice opposition between that advert idea and long-locked hippie Suzanne. And Betty with her hair in rollers. And Paul casting a longing look back at the good old days of the Jackie v Marilyn opposition as blonde Betty and dark-haired Suzanne resist that binary equation, and not only does Peggy render it meaningless to her role in the workplace, but Don's secretary refuses to go to the ball with Ken.

EPISODE 11: The Gypsy And The Hobo

"We got a gypsy and a hobo. And who are you supposed to be?" CARLTON HANSON

If last week was all about the discovery, tonight was all about the unravelling. After some testing questions from Betty – she asks Don for more money, knowing full well that he has thousands of dollars upstairs – it seems like her chance to confront him may have passed. But with the kids and Betty supposedly away at William's, an oblivious Don pops back to Bullet Park Road to pick some bits up for his trip with Suzanne – only to bump into Betty. Who finally makes him reveal all. We saw a new Betty here, she's finally got all the power ("You don't get to ask any questions") and as she reveals that she knows the contents of the drawer, you see the construct of "Don Draper" disappear immediately from Dick Whitman's eyes; a ghost exorcised.

It's testament to the plotting so far that this grand storyline doesn't feel dragged out – and also that we feel almost equal sympathy for Don and Betty. As Don says: when could he have told her? When do you break open a lie that big? But we understand Betty's anger too. The affairs are small fry compared to this – he has forced a stranger's name upon her. It's an incredibly painful couple of scenes – we see Don too shaky to hold a cigarette; the threat of Suzanne wandering in any minute; the confession about leaving Adam to hang himself. By the end of his mea culpa there are signs that Betty feels for him – a gentle hand on the shoulder – but her silent demeanour at breakfast the next day suggests that even he might not be able to wriggle out of this one. Was she in denial, though – did she really think Don was just "some football hero who hated his father" all this time?

The trick-or-treating scene that followed did a wonderful job of framing this for them. With Sally and Bobby dressed as mini Don and Bettys – a gypsy queen and a nomadic hobo – it was left to Francine's husband Carlton to ask the question that Don's been asking himself for over a decade – "Who are you supposed to be?"

"The closest we got to Hemingway was sitting in a chair he once sat in." ANNABELLE MATHIS

While Don is in the process of having his present defenestrated, Roger's past catches up with him, as an old lover comes into the office over the rebranding of her pony-meat dog food. We learn that Caldecott Farms' Annabelle Mathis left Roger in the 1940s for her husband. She broke his heart but has regretted it ever since. Roger – who seems like he's fronting – insists that despite their wonderful memories of Paris he's over her. He proves it at the restaurant, rejecting her drunken advance out of loyalty to Jane. I'm not sure if this proves Roger has changed particularly, but combined with the scene with Joan it does paint him in a more serious tone than we're used to – the firm loses the account but Roger wins our respect and, for once, appears as more than a "character in somebody else's novel".

"You don't know what it's like to want something your whole life ... and not get it." GREG HARRIS

Joan, however, has other issues besides asking Roger for a job. Despite her help with Greg's psychiatry interview (she'd clearly make a better one than him), he can't make the leap from inept surgeon to inept headshrinker and fluffs his lines once more: "I did everything I was supposed to do!" he cries. After taking his frustration out on Joan and getting a vase around the head for his troubles (take that Kowalski!) he decides that the best recourse is an army surgeon job where he figures he'll be based in NYC and "maybe Vietnam if that's still going on".

NOTES

- The Hofstadt family lawyer's advice to Betty (stay put) showed how archaic the divorce laws in New York were – unless Don was physically abusive or adultrous she will have trouble getting anything from him. This, like the battle for Gene's house with William, could get messy. If only she knew a lawyer ...

- Surely the vase would have at least knocked Greg out – if not killed him?

- Don has eaten horse meat. Presumably a byproduct of his poverty – it cost half the price of beef. In the same scene we see Don lighting up just as Annabelle tells Roger her husband died of lung cancer.

- Don and Suzanne were supposed to be off to 19th century seaport Mystic, Connecticut.

CULTURE WATCH

- The mustangs-into-dog-food plot of John Huston's The Misfits is the reason for Caldecott Farms' woes.

- Annabel and Roger bonded over Casablanca (1942) before Sterling left for the Pacific.

- The closing music is of Where Is Love? from Oliver!, drawing a line between lost orphans Whitman and Twist. Is there a link between the tragic half brothers Dick and Adam Whitman and Dickens's Monks and Oliver too?

THOUGHTS FROM THE TYPING POOL

JoeDoone Despite herself, Betty is sympathetic [when she finds out], not least of all because she knows that this is the real man talking. He is being completely honest with her, for the first time; he even tells her about Adam's suicide. The only thing he hasn't told her about is Suzanne; the proof of adultery Betty's lawyer talked about is sitting out in the car.

Shov Don dropping the cigarette mirrored Dick dropping his lighter back when he became Don. Wonder how long it takes for the flames to reach the depot?

Dominia Jon Hamm's finest moment, what a tour de force. And despite the gut-wrenching soul bearing, Don's PR skills have not entirely deserted him. He edits the crucial detail of how the identity switch was accomplished, claiming he was injured and it was the army's mistake. His act may be against the law, but this embellishment softens the ethical impact considerably.

Insomniac506 Betty's been able to live for all these years knowing nothing about her husband's past life, not meeting any of his friends, presumably defending him to her family who mistrusted him, and not delving into the Secret Drawer even though she's known it's always been there. We learned a little about what Betty had guessed about Don – that he was poor and ashamed of it – and one wonders about what Betty had invested in saying nothing and keeping quiet. Partially it's because Don wouldn't tell her anything, but she also seems to have been attracted to his mysteriousness and lack of backstory.

MacEasy I thought explicitly of Hitchcock, and it was that drawer scene which did it for me. A classic Hitch strategy, investing an object such as the keys and the drawer with such loaded symbolism – perhaps an inheritance of his from silent film, but one which also plays into his obsessions with guilt, transference, secrets and discovery. And of course Betty, as others have noted, looks in these scenes like a quintessential Hitchcock blonde.

RockNRollMassacre With Greg becoming a psychiatrist, there is also a beautifully played out little bit of Freudian theory in action this week, with Don's secret box and lost key working out as a text book example of the Return of the Repressed. As Betty points out – Don (subconsciously) wanted her to find out. People have mentioned Lacan in the past here too, and I can't help but notice there's a mental health consultant [Hilary Jacobs Hendel] listed in the credits.

KeithyD At last the Great American Theme comes crawling, blinking, from the wreckage of Don and Betty's marriage: the nature of identity. From Dick – sorry, Walt – Whitman's "I contain multitudes" to Moby Dick's narrator's request – "Call me Ishmael" – the question is, how do you create an identity in an ever-changing world in which there are no fixed certainties?

Don's Gatsby-esque front (never so obvious as when discussing his previous life of poverty with rich girl Betty/Daisy) finally crumbles. His identity is bound up with his name – he's 'draped' himself with another's history, wife, son and, so far as we know, job. When the name is proved to be a lie, so does his identity. How ironic that he tells the dog-food queen, of her brand-name: "It's a label on a can," which possibly reflects the ease with which he himself made the switch. Of course she replies, "That name got us where we are," so perhaps she's more aware of the level of integrity embodied in it than he. Because he has got where he is as Don Draper, not Dick Whitman.

The theme of identity is echoed elsewhere, too: Joan's husband looking to be *given* a role, having done everything he was "supposed" to do up until then. And finally finding one in the army, where his lack of personality will probably enable him to move right on up.

Digit Advertising is all in the service of the Big Other, the transcendent authority that, of course, has no real existence, but that is nevertheless used to structure our existences and desires: such and such is what we're supposed to want; such and such is what we're supposed to do to get it, etc. As poor Dr Greg says this episode, "I did everything I was supposed to do!" Everything the Big Other told him to, in other words.

The Drapers, as a storybook 50s family, are the paradigm of the objective laid down by the era's collective sense of the Big Other: the couple on the top of the wedding cake, Ken and Barbie, etc. It's no accident that they keep being compared to dolls. "The woman does not exist," says Lacan. Slavoj Zizek's gloss on this (if I remember rightly) is that the woman, as repository for the man's desire, is the ultimate *objet petit a*, the fetish spuriously invested with meaning, the attainment of which is supposed to be the rendering of the man's identity: hence, the man does not exist either. Don Draper, who literally does not exist, seeks to make himself real in the world through the impossible blond bombshell 50s ideal woman who is Betty. They succeed in creating the image, but cannot invest it with the required meaning. Don ends up, "scratching at [his] own life".

Oldmuskrat All I can say is that Don was very lucky that Suzanne wasn't honking the car horn outside.

EPISODE 12: The Grown Ups

"He was so handsome and now I'll never get to vote for him." JANE

We've often discussed Mad Men's skill at deftly weaving real world events together with its fiction. But in The Grown Ups, as we all expected, action in the real world brutally invades the narrative one. John F Kennedy's shooting derails Margaret's wedding and provides the end of the worldliness (see Culture Watch) that prompts several of the characters to consider their own existence.

The handling of Dallas was superb, with the slow drip of information gradually reaching all the ensemble as they watch Walter Cronkite break the news. The tears of Carla and Betty seemed real and the two appear close for once, despite seemingly grieving for different ideals (though JFK was no civil rights evangelist, he was a key player in pushing through the Civil Rights Act).

The best of Roger is showcased too as he does his level best to hold it together while his daughter's wedding falls apart. Jane, notably, can't tear herself away from the TV and by the end of the evening is drunk again. The telephone chat – with Mona translating his anger to Margaret – was a touching look at their old complementary parenting styles and, of course, his ringing "Red" at the end of the night to get a bit of perspective hints back to the last episode's mentions of his true love.

The combination of the wedding and the assassination seemed to trigger introspection in others, too …

"Take a pill and lie down, I can handle the kids." DON

After waking up to find a shamed Don holding baby Gene, we wonder if Betty's going to forgive him his indiscretions, but everything – as she later clarifies – now seems cold to her. The marriage is bust. At Margaret's wedding Betty is reluctant to kiss and dance with Don – her only enjoyment of the evening comes from realising that the girl with Henry is his daughter, not his wife. Three weeks have passed since she found out about Dick Whitman, but with JFK acting as an avatar for her grief for her marriage (and her father), and having been reminded of her feelings for Henry (having finally got her kiss), she knows she's not in love any more. Camelot is over in Ossining and Washington DC.

Twice Don says – as much to himself as Betty and the kids – that "everything's going to be all right". But the dead look he gets from his wife as he leaves for work on the day of the funeral suggests otherwise. The "I don't love you" moment, in which Betty is admirably restrained in trying to articulate what Don has done to her, is made compelling by Don's refusal to understand. He tries to pass her off like an annoyed client, hoping she'll see the solidity of his campaign, but that trick doesn't work any more. We see the shift in power through the couple's role-reversal – Betty leaving Don at home without explanation to see her paramour, while Don punts the kids off to Francine's. Betty's holding all the aces – and with no bars open all Don can do is mope into work.

"I know a nooner when I hear one." KINSEY

Also in the office with no particular place to go is, predictably, Peggy who has been forced out of her flat by perky housemate Karen and annoyed by her mother's grief-hogging. As soon as we see Don walking into an empty office, we know the sound of click-clacking keys in the distance are coming from her typewriter. She's also been busy with Duck who was more interested in a lunchtime quickie than finding out if the president is still alive. Meanwhile, the catty chat she had after lunch with Karen – "I don't see why a lunch counter is any better than eating at your desk" – proves that she's not quite got the hang of playing the bright young Manhattanite just yet.

"I found out yesterday that head of accounts is going to Kenny and his haircut." PETE

Pete's going nowhere, too. He's cornered into a new title, working under "Kenny" Cosgrove who, as Lane puts it, "has the rare gift of making clients feel as if they haven't any needs". Perhaps fortunately for Pete, his problems are put into perspective by events in Dallas. It does appear as though he's using it as an excuse not to go to the wedding, though – since when is Campbell the type to be offended by bottom-line merchants like Harry? But his sense of entitlement is still unjustified. While Peggy gets her head down and improves after being treated unfairly, Pete rachets up the melodrama and tells Trudy "I got fired". He whinnies so much that it's Trudy, rather than Pete, who articulates his desire to leave. Will he have the balls to do it? Interestingly, Trudy echoes Greg (in the previous episode) when she tells him: "You did everything they asked you to do." Life isn't fair. Ask Jackie Kennedy.

NOTES

- I wouldn't mind Roger making a toast at my wedding: "Mona, you're a lioness, thank you for resisting the urge to eat your cub."

- Pete may have his faults, but he knows an instant hot cocoa when he tastes one.

- The conflict between Margaret and Jane is intriguing. But if you marry a father figure, expect sibling rivalry: "Everything you do is for her," complains Jane.

20TH CENTURY TALES

- When Betty is asleep Henry Francis's man Rockefeller is talking on the radio discussing JFK.

CULTURE WATCH

- Pete tells Trudy "Stop it with the Ellery Queen". As in the detective mag Ellery Queen's Mystery Magazine.
- Betty's favourite movie is one from her prom queen youth – Singin' In The Rain (1952).
- The credits song is Skeeter Davis's The End Of The World. While America is contemplating the end of one world, Don is wondering if his sun will go on shining.

THOUGHTS FROM THE TYPING POOL

SboobyDoo Cronkite's report may be the iconic one that usually turns up in shows and movies covering the aftermath of the assassination, but the secretaries turned from Cronkite's broadcast to the Huntley-Brinkley Report, which was the more popular news programme of the time.

DogManStar The scene where Betty and Carla were watching the news with an uncomprehending Sally trying to comfort her mom is unbearably moving.

I can't believe I didn't twig at the time (in Kinsey Theatre) that Peggy's Aqua Net commercial [the problems of an open-top car] was about to become the most unsuitable in advertising history.

JoeDoone As the end music tells us, it is the end of the world in many ways. Betty, whose world was shattered last week by Don's many lies, blames him for distorting how she feels about the murder of the president. She tells Don: "I don't know where to begin. I want to scream at you for ruining all this, but then you try to fix it, and there's no point. I don't love you. I don't love you any more. I kissed you yesterday; I didn't feel a thing. You can't even hear me right now."

Insomniac506 This episode delivered dazzlingly well, both in showing how the events of history can both be life changing, and at the same time just provide a backdrop or a distraction for our own personal crises. The first signs we see of the assassination happen in the background while poor put-on petulant Pete has a sulky conversation with Harry Crane about his career prospects. Was anyone else screaming "Look behind you?" at the screen like I was?

This episode may well have redeemed Roger's reputation. He managed to deal with both his children, Margaret and Jane, who locked herself in the bathroom a la Zelda Fitzgerald. His wedding speech was perfect, and his acknowledgement of Mona was probably the most honourable thing he's done all season. And my heart broke with his conversation with "Red". Roger and Joan are soulmates – something Roger is just realising, which is why he's calling her and not his 21-year-old wife who's passed out in bed next to him.

KeithyD Of course this episode wasn't about Kennedy at all. It was brilliant the way that the assassination was used as a metaphor for the end of Don and Betty's marriage. It was a rupture, a seismic shock, a paradigm shift. After the shock of the assassination, the end of their marriage seems perfectly reasonable, because now anything is possible. The assassination has changed the rules of the game. The 60s are possible. Nothing is fixed.

RocknRollMassacre I think it was *hugely* telling that when she saw the news, Carla sat down on the sofa next to Betty and lit a cigarette. The effect of what they were seeing on television was that they were made equals, that there was a complete change in how they related to each other, which wasn't said, but which was made entirely evident.

LondonPony Was the wedding guests' gathering in the hotel kitchen a nod forward to RFK's assassination?

SuperSpartan Was the dancing at the wedding meant to be contrasted with the last time we saw them all dancing, at Roger's country club? There seem so many links: Roger holding ceremony, the connection between Henry and Betty, Jane getting drunk, etc. But a couple of stark contrasts, aside from the general mood – the difference in the relationship between Don and Betty at the end of each dance; Pete and Trudy's joyous scene stealing at the club and their sad absence from the dancing at the wedding.

KeithyD Pete and Trudy are the show's avatars of the 60s to come. Pete seems to be being radicalised by what's happening around him – the death of his father focuses him on the fact that he has to stand alone now, which includes thinking independently. He's one of the few on the show to really be aware of what's going on in society. His family background perhaps also gives him the spine to be able to stand up to other social pressures to conform in order to think his own thoughts. I'd guess a lot of social change in the US in the 60s came from the radicalised middle- and upper-classes (all those white folks on Dr King's marches), not just from a disempowered working-class. Trudy seems to be soaking up some of Pete's attitude – perhaps initially from the perspective of supporting "her man", but also from a growing realisation that she can have an opinion too.

DellaMirandola What about Pete's line about how he thought it looked as if things were really going to change and now with Johnson they are back to more of the same – little does he know …

EPISODE 13: Shut The Door, Have A Seat

So we end the series with the two divorces of Donald Francis Draper. One from the love of his life, and the other from his wife. With Don's personal travails having been so predominant over the last 13 episodes, the end of Sterling Cooper as we know it gave us some fun respite.

"Well gentleman, I suppose you're fired." LANE

Conrad Hilton's role in this series has been an odd one, but tonight illustrates his importance – he's been a catalyst in so much of the narrative and he's the one who gives Don an early tip about the projected PPL sale. The resultant turmoil – which spells out why Draper was so determined not to sign a contract – results in Don (who's busy flashing back to the self-sufficiency of his tragic father) trying to persuade Roger and Bert to join him in buying back the firm. Pryce fires the three of them to release them from their contracts, before being fired himself for the act of doing so. But not before Roger and Pete have nabbed tens of millions of dollars' worth of clients first.

The Sunday night "carpet cleaning", and the (predictable?) return of Joan provided a giddy finale – but the best scenes were those of a humbled but back-in-the-saddle Don having to pay the dues he owes to Roger, Pete and Peggy. He tries once with Peggy in the way he always has, assuming she'll go with him, but Peggy knows her value and stands up to him. Later Don visits her apartment to say something so out of character that she is almost in tears: "I don't know if I can do it alone – will you help me?"

Pete also plays hardball but overplays his hand somewhat, before Don admits Pete's worth to them and he quickly agrees to join. And there was some great banter with Bert ("If you've lost your appetite") before Don and Roger coalesce 1960-style in the bar. And then "just when things were back to normal", he inadvertently drops Betty in it.

So while Harry (SCDP's head of media, no less) is in with whizkids Peggy and Pete, Cosgrove and Kinsey and everyone else are out. Ken is one of my favourite minor characters so it's been disappointing seeing him reduced to a one-liner-spouting aside this season. He seems better at his job than Pete too. Yes Pete might have been on the money with aeronautics etc but is that a strong enough reason (besides narrative necessity) for Pete to remain? Will SCDP need an art director and a pompous faux-liberal too?

"You said you'd always come home." SALLY

Meanwhile, Don's other divorce is much more painful. But just as final. When Betty tells hims she's made an appointment with an attorney he tries to give her the "take a pill and lie down" approach that might have worked three years ago, but didn't work last episode and won't work now. We see Don moving from this denial, to the anger of his confrontation with Betty over Henry ("all the while long, you've been building a life raft") to the acceptance of his final phone call. In this he seems aware of his failings – it's not about nice houses in the suburbs, it's about love. And it doesn't live in Bullet Park road anymore.

This denouement is a good one, for all involved. Bobby and Sally haven't lived in a family for years. Don can be a tender father, but he's an absent bastard most of the time. Let's hope that he's got the decency to stay in their lives. The talk in the living room was the saddest of them all. The incomprehension of Bobby, the near-comprehension of Sally who was angry at her father ("you say things and you don't mean them") before shifting the blame onto her mother. "Did you make him leave?" she asks.

But as Betty heads with Gene and Henry to Reno, let's not forget her and her friends' mockery of divorcee Helen Bishop in series one. What goes around …

NOTES

- Great to see Don with the bit between his teeth again. Prepare for some Lucky Strike/Kodak Carousel-style magic in season four.

- How did Pete get Clearasil back? An excited Trudy leaning on her father?

- The door to the art department had an "f" stuck in front of the "a".

- It was a nice touch that Bobby assumes Sally and he are in trouble because they're in the living room – which is obviously never used

- Don to Peggy on the changing of the tides: "There are people out there who buy things. And something happened, something terrible and the way that they saw themselves is gone. And nobody understands that. But you do. And that's very valuable."

- Why does Betty have to go for a quickie Reno divorce – can't she threaten Don with exposure of his affairs? Or is that moot now that he knows about Henry?

CULTURE WATCH

- "The future is much better than the past," sings Roy Orbison in Shahdaroba as the end credits play. Quite.

- The "you're a whore" scene in the Draper's bedroom was similar to a scene at the climax of Cheever's Bullet Park: "It (the marriage) was an eight-year mess. He drank and accused me of having affairs with other men and wrote anonymous letters to most of my friends claiming I had the principles of a whore. I bought him off, I had to, I paid him a shirtful and went off to Reno. I came back last month."

THOUGHTS FROM THE TYPING POOL

MacEasy "The way that they saw themselves is gone," – Mad Men is the only TV drama that I can think of that is so reflective about itself and its characters, and that remark, inserted in a painful admission from Don, is typically embedded in a conversation about something else (winning Peggy back to the new firm), but could stand for the trajectory the entire series has been taking.

JoeDoone Betty must be soft in the head to trust Henry and his "you don't want to owe Don" routine – in other words, let Don walk off with his assets intact, and she is totally dependent upon Henry. Why not enjoy the freedom to make her own future, rather than repeat past mistakes?

Riverangel When Don said to Betty "You're a whore," my sense of her unspoken thought was "like your mother" and the fact she then did hold the baby boy gave that moment a kind of karmic symmetry.

Nevada The whole episode was about the future and who was going with it and who was left behind: the death of one dream and the start of another. The transformation of so many people was wonderful to see: Pete's face when Roger and Don visit – the way he's standing to attention in his dressing gown like a little boy facing an angry father only to turn into an adult glowing with a sense of his new worth. Peggy's interactions with Don were perfect and reflected back to their, again, private moments about their personal fears.

DellaMirandola I really hope Paul and Ken come back, if only for a catch-up. Ken can take care of himself but poor Paul: he started out on the same level as Pete, Ken and Harry, and now Ken is going to be head of accounts, Harry has his own department, and Pete and Peggy have been poached because of their brilliance (no-one could poach Harry because of his brilliance: loved him sitting by himself in the hotel bedroom). Maybe Paul will write a bitter expose of the advertising world (The Frauds of Madison Avenue: A Personal Journey Into the Dark Heart Of The American Dream).

GoddessInTheBlueSari Don seems finally to have made peace with his father. Conrad Hilton pulls no punches with essentially the same message (though less viciously meant) as Don's dad. Don is galvanised into action after the flashback of seeing Archie Whitman determined to go it alone. It was tender to see the young Dick Whitman distressed and bent over his dad's dead body. The renewed, dynamic Don is a chip off the old block after all.

HelenaOfTroy Despite the monumental plot progression in this episode, what really stood out was the Peggy-Don relationship. As Don is leaving both his children and his father figures behind, he reaches out to Peggy, who has always looked up to him as a mentor and shows her the chink in his armour.

NoseyRosey Loved the bank heist style dénouement. From the the music, to putting the "team" together to pull off the job, to Pete leaving with rifle over his shoulder like an armed robber. Then the next morning the "we've been robbed!" shock, confusion in the Manhattan office and bellowing fury in London. Also, the shape of the fatal horseshoe was grotesquely imprinted on Dick/Don's father's face. Subsequently, the [Ad Age award won in series one] award sitting behind Don is a horseshoe set on a wooden plaque.

Discussant But the horseshoe isn't strictly unlucky for Don. As in life, the good and the bad are intertwined – to be a fully integrated person, Don needed his past to return. The horseshoe award brought his brother back. This led to his brother's suicide and Don learns the true cost of repression. The horseshoe killed Don's father: this led to Don realizing that if he tried to go it alone, he was doomed. He needed to move forward in life by mending his relationships and, in effect, creating a new co-op with Cooper, Sterling, Pryce, Pete, and Peggy.

The complete Mad Men playlist

SEASON ONE
Title Sequence:
RJD2 – Beautiful Mine (Instrumental Version)

Episode 1:
Band of Gold by Don Cherry
Shangri-La by Robert Maxwell
Caravan by Gordon Jenkins
The Street Where You Live by Vic Damone & Percy Faith

Episode 2:
I Can Dream Can't I by the Andrews Sisters
The Great Divide by the Cardigans

Episode 3:
PS I Love You by Bobby Vinton

Episode 4:
Driving Instructor (Comedy Bit) by Bob Newhart
Manhattan by Ella Fitzgerald

Episode 5:
Blue in Green by Miles Davis
You by the Aquatones
Non Dimenticar by Percy Faith

Episode 6:
Babylon (by Don McLean) by the cast

Episode 7:
There Will Never Be Another You by Bud Powell
Night and Day by Luiz Bonfa
Botch-A-Me (Ba-Ba-Baciami Piccina) by Rosemary Clooney

Episode 8:
Concierto De Aranjuez (Adagio) by Miles Davis
Choo Choo Cha Cha by Rinky Dink
The Twist by Chubby Checker

Episode 9:
My Special Angel by Bobby Helms

Episode 10:
Volare by the McGuire Sisters

Episode 11:
Agua de Beber by Astrud Gilberto
Fly Me to the Moon by Julie London

Episode 12:
Gopher Mambo by Yma Sumac
Metro Polka by Frankie Laine

Episode 13:
Don't Think Twice, It's Alright by Bob Dylan

SEASON TWO
Episode 1:
Let's Twist Again by Chubby Checker
Song Of The Indian Guest by Rimsky-Korsakov

Episode 2:
Congratulations Honey by Baby Washington & The Plants
Temptation Is Hard to Fight by George McGregor & The
Bronzettes
Sukiaki by Kyo Sakamoto

Episode 3:
Lollipops & Roses by Jack Jones

Episode 4:
The Blue Room by Perry Como

Episode 5:
Theme From A Summer's Place by Percy Faith and his Orchestra

Episode 6:
The Infanta by the Decemberists

Episode 7:
I'm In Love by the Pentagons
Break it to Me Gently by Brenda Lee

Episode 8:
Early in the Morning by Peter, Paul & Mary

Episode 9:
Pot Can't Talk About the Kettle by Helene Smith
I'm Through with Love by Marilyn Monroe

Episode 10:
Swingin' Saints by the Gigalos
Telstar by the Tornados

Episode 11:
What'll I Do? by Johnny Mathis

Episode 12:
Treat You Right by the Sevilles
Cup of Loneliness by George Jones

Episode 13:
Stranger On the Shore by Acker Bilk

SEASON THREE
Episode 2:
Bye Bye Birdie by Ann-Margret
To Be Loved by the Pentagons

Episode 3:
Memories Of You by Ben Webster

Episode 6:
Come On Twist by Jody Reynolds
Song to Woody by Bob Dylan

Episode 7:
Darling Say You Love Me by the Ramblers
I Followed My Heart by Pete Mann
Sixteen Tons by Tennessee Ernie Ford

Episode 8:
There's A Small Hotel by Bobby Van and Kay Coulter

Episode 13:
Shahdaroba by Roy Orbison

Source: AMC